MILITARY RETIREMENT

A MODERN GUIDE TO NAVIGATING THE ARMY RETIREMENT SYSTEM

BY
LIEUTENANT COLONEL BRIAN PARKER
US ARMY, RET

<u>Works Available by Brian Parker</u>

Amazon Link for Brian's works:
<u>http://hyperurl.co/49bffn</u>

<u>American Dreams series</u>
The Decline | *The Ascent* | *End Game*

<u>Five Roads to Texas series</u>
Five Roads to Texas | *After the Roads* | *The Road to Hell*
The Days Before (a prequel) | *Reciprocity*

<u>Easytown Novels</u>
The Immorality Clause | *Tears of a Clone*
West End Droids & East End Dames | *House of the Rising*
Gun | *High Tech/Low Life: An Easytown Anthology*

<u>The Path of Ashes series</u>
A Path of Ashes | *Fireside* | *Dark Embers*

<u>Washington, Dead City series</u>
GNASH | *REND* | *SEVER*

<u>Stand Alone Works</u>
Grudge | *Enduring Armageddon*
Origins of the Outbreak | *The Collective Protocol*
Battle Damage Assessment | *Zombie in the Basement*

<u>Non Fiction</u>
Self-Publishing the Hard Way
Military Retirement: A Modern Guide to Navigating the
Military Retirement System
Plus, many more anthology contributions and short
stories.

CONTENTS

FOREWORD

As I neared my retirement, I thought there would be a set process for how to do this. You know, a checklist of everything that needs to be done. The Army lives and breathes by checklists, guidelines, and standards. There are literally tens of thousands of soldiers who go through the retirement process every year. There *has* to be a checklist, right? Wrong.

Okay, that's not necessarily true, there is an Army Retirement Guide that's updated each year. It wasn't particularly helpful for me. Also, I don't mean to disparage the good folks at Retirement Services who deal with a hundred completely different issues on a daily basis, however, there's a reason I wrote this retirement guide. If you catch my drift. Luckily for you, I've created a checklist at the end of this guide. If you find yourself with very little time to read this entire guide, the checklist may be just what you need.

While we're going to discuss the steps and ways to go about your retirement process, I would be remiss if I didn't address the elephant in the room: Are you *prepared* to retire? I'm not talking about if you're *ready* to do so, I think most folks begin to feel the draw around the 15-year mark. Are you actually prepared to do so, financially, mentally, socially, etc.? In addition to taking that giant leap of faith that you'll be able to support yourself and your family, you will also be stepping away from two-plus decades of a built-in support system that you might not have really appreciated for what it was. Just think on that as you go through this process.

As you've neared your retirement date, you've likely been playing around on the Army Retirement website looking at the calculators, and just generally getting the lay of the land for a few *years* before you were eligible to begin the process. It's normal. You're not letting your soldiers down or as one senior officer told me when I dropped my paperwork, "quitting." You're doing the right thing for you and you're also thinking about beginning to pass the torch onto the next generation. You won't always be there to be the subject matter expert, and here's a secret: the Army will be just fine without you. It will continue to perform its duty of protecting our nation's population, our sovereign territories, and our foreign interests.

I've seen too many soldiers who didn't prepare properly and were rushed to get everything done in the time allotted. The Army will keep working you until the day you retire **if you let them**. This may sound harsh to a hard-charging soldier who's always been looked after (or not) by their senior leadership; nobody is looking out for you in retirement, except you. I had the benefit of being in DC for my transition and seeing all of the retirees at

Bethesda/Walter Reed. The retirees go in there wearing their old rank badges on their Army Veteran hats and sit in the prescription waiting room for their meds. And yes, I've seen several retired general officers that I recognized treated the same as everyone else. When you retire, you are no longer the [insert super-important duty title here], you're just another retiree. Prepare for that now and don't let it surprise you the first time it happens.

I'm not trying to be all doom and gloom, though, because retirement is glorious! I'm just throwing out that reminder that *how* you prepare for your retirement can help to set you up for success after you transition.

This guide is directed at military retirement, however, probably 90 percent of the information can be used for those servicemembers who ETS after their term of service is over. In fact, the Army had single-term enlistment and soldiers who were being administratively separated enrolled in the same SFL-TAP classes that I took. It was a good experience to have people at various stages of their career and the perspectives they brought with them in the classes together since that's exactly what the mix will be in your post-service career—if you choose to work, that is.

One interesting thing that needs to be highlighted up front to set the scene for the future military retiree is that almost nothing is set in stone, which is absolutely crazy when we've made our careers adhering to rules and regulations. What one person tells you can be completely different than what another person says. I can only tell you what happened with me and what worked, and what didn't. I don't claim to have every bit of information for you, however, I hope this guide will help you navigate some of the pitfalls associated with your retirement from the US military.

As I began the retirement process, I discovered immediately that that there's no "one size fits all" solution, and everything for me was discovery learning. Other installations may have a rock-solid plan of attack, a way ahead, the proverbial checklist if you will, but not the one I retired from. This guide evolved out of a series of emails to colleagues as I went through the process. I kept the emails and now that I'm about six months into retirement, set up with the Department of Veterans Affairs, and working at a second career, I feel that it's time to put everything I learned to paper to help people going through the same issues that I'd experienced.

As an established fiction author, I felt that I could spend some time and help my fellow servicemembers out by writing a no-BS guide based on **my personal experiences**. This is not meant to be the one size fits all approach that my Retirement Services office said was impossible to create. It is simply information to help you out along the way, written by someone with recent experience.

I want to point out that I may use Army terminology or reference Army programs throughout this guide. That doesn't mean that the guide is only for Soldiers. Our sister services don't always speak the same language, but it should be more than enough to get you started on your journey.

This guide isn't going to read like some Army Regulation or Field Manual, I write as I speak, and military jargon has never really been my thing. It's in plain, everyday English that we all should be able to understand. Also, this is very important: I am not a lawyer or a financial advisor! Make sure you speak to both before you plan to retire.

Oh yeah, congratulations on your retirement! It's been a long, arduous journey, full of ups and downs. Be proud of your service to our great nation and thank you for everything that you've done!

Brian Parker, LTC (Ret)

YOUR RETIREMENT PACKET

So, how the heck do you start the process of retirement and what do you expect to happen during it? That's the whole reason you picked up this guide, right? Of course it is. I mention in other places in this guide, the retirement process is not linear. You'll have several requirements with different agencies going on simultaneously. There's no exact "this is where you start" moment, so I'll begin with explaining the process and how you go about the paperwork side of the house first, even though you may actually be conducting other steps prior to dropping your retirement packet.

The biggest takeaway from my recent experience is that the Army retirement process is like a 3-legged stool. The legs are held onto the seat by duct tape and none of the legs want anything to do with the others. The three legs of the so-called Retirement Stool are: the Soldier For Life—Transition Assistance Program (SFL-TAP), Retirement Services—which switches over to the Transition Services branch after your Survivor Benefit Plan (SBP) election, and Military Medical. The military medical and VA healthcare are somewhat linked, but completely separate…so maybe a 4-legged stool that one leg has fallen off of it is more appropriate.

Like a good staff officer, I've made a PowerPoint chart to illustrate the Army retirement process:

As I mentioned in my foreword, the retirement process isn't linear, and an attempt to explain it that way would fail miserably. You'll have several different processes running simultaneously that you'll need to keep track of. While the very first items you can begin working on are your medical and SFL-TAP requirements, for ease of flow, I'm going to begin with your retirement packet, or the Army's process for "dropping your paperwork," and what this life-altering decision means to you and your family.

The Packet

Human Resources Command (HRC) actually doesn't require a whole lot of paperwork from you. Your installation and unit, however, will be the proverbial death by a thousand cuts. Every time you turn around, it seems like your S-1 or some random person at the installation will need some new document or form from you. Don't get frustrated, just keep your eyes on the prize: that sweet, sweet DD214.

HRC's retirement pages are pretty worthless, in my opinion. When preparing information for this guide, I could only find the Enlisted Retirements and Separation Branch page, and the only thing there was pointing you to a regulation…boring. They do have a checklist for you, though, if you're being involuntarily separated. Geez. Here's the one page I could find any information:

https://www.hrc.army.mil/content/Regular%20Army%20Enlisted%20Retirements%20and%20Separations

The S-1 folks at your unit should have a list of the documents required for your initial retirement request. For the purpose of this guide, I'm going to rely on those emails that I provided fellow soldiers when I was going through the retirement process. This is the only part of the retirement process where there may be differences between how an officer requests retirement versus an enlisted soldier. Again, your S-1 should have the information you need.

If you fail to send in your retirement request 9-12 months out from your requested retirement date, you'll have to include a letter of lateness from the first O-5 in your chain of command. I've seen plenty of soldiers rush through and get it submitted late, but none of them have had a peaceful transition. So, do yourself a favor and submit the packet 12 months out. Remember how I told you that the Army will work you right up until the end if you let them? They will. Especially soldiers in leadership positions. I've known many battalion commanders and command sergeant majors who were still going to the field and galivanting around the globe on TDY during the time they were supposed to be taking for themselves to retire. I saw one of our squadron commanders at medical one day during my retirement process. He was supposed to retire the same month that I did. He was so far behind and completely stressed out (as much as a dude from Hawaii can be at least) because neither he nor his family had gotten the time to wind down. It was go-go-go right up until about one month out from his transition leave time. You know what? I'm sure the unit said that he was a good guy after he retired. I'm also sure the next commander who came along changed everything and he was soon forgotten. While the Army will move along without you, you've only got one shot at making your transition a successful one. When it's time to drop your paperwork, you need to purposefully step back and let someone else do the heavy lifting.

At a minimum, your retirement packet must consist of the following:

- MFR on unit letterhead stating your intention to retire (for officers). Here's an example:

Office Symbol   DATE

MEMORANDUM THRU Commander, Unit Address

MEMORANDUM FOR Chief, Retirement Services Branch, Installation

SUBJECT: Voluntary Retirement – Name., Rank, Branch

1. Under the provisions of law cited in AR 600-8-24, paragraph 6-1 and MILPER 14-308, I request that I be released from active duty and assignment on [31 Month 202X] and placed on the retired list on [01 Month 202X], or as soon thereafter as practicable. I will have completed over [XX] years of active Federal service on the requested retirement date.

2. Assignment status: Unit and address

3. Authorized place of retirement: Installation

4. Location of choice transition activity: Installation

5. I have been counseled as specified by AR 635-10, paragraph 2-19. I fully understand the provisions of AR 635-10, chapter 2, section V, concerning entitlement to per diem, travel and transportation allowances based on retirement at a location of choice transition activity.

6. I have read AR 600-8-24, paragraph 6-6 and 6-7. I am responsible for insuring that a physical examination is completed not earlier than 4 months nor later than one month prior to my approved retirement date (subject physical to be arranged through coordination with my unit of assignment) or start date of transition leave, whichever is earlier. I am aware that the purpose of this examination is to insure that my medical records reflect as accurately as possible my state of health on retirement and to protect my interests and those of the Government. I also understand that my retirement will take effect on the requested date and that I will not be held on active duty to complete this examination.

7. In accordance with 10 USC, I understand that—

    a. Enrollment in the Survivor Benefit Plan (SBP) is the only way that I may continue a portion of my retirement pay to my family at my death.

> b. I must receive SBP counseling for myself and my spouse no less than 60 days before my retirement.
>
> c. I will be enrolled in full SBP coverage if I fail to elect otherwise in writing before my retirement.
>
> d. I cannot elect less than full spouse SBP without my spouse's written agreement. My spouse will receive a spousal concurrence for this purpose. I realize there are other forms that must be completed during SBP counseling.
>
> e. Failure to return the completed spousal concurrence statement to the proper officials prior to my retirement packet being set to the Defense Finance and Accounting Center will result in my being irrevocable and irreversibly enrolled in SBP at full cost.
>
> 8. Address upon retirement: Home address
>
> 9. I am familiar with AR 600-8-24, paragraph 6-22, and understand that if this application for retirement is accepted by the Secretary of the Army it may not be withdrawn except for extreme compassionate reasons or for the definitely established convenience of the Government.
>
> 10. As of the date of this application, I have [XX] days accrued leave. I do plan to take transition leave. I plan to take [XX] days transition leave. I plan to take 20 days PTDY from [Date—Date].
>
> 11. I have read and understand the provisions of AR 600-8-24, table 6-2 or 6-2, pertaining to determination of my retired grade. Considering those provisions, and after a review of my records, I believe that I am entitled to retire in the grade of [PAY GRADE]. I understand that final determination of my retired grade will be made by HQDA, and that I will be informed if I am not entitled to retire in the grade I have specified in this paragraph.
>
> 12. This application is submitted in lieu of involuntary separation.
>
> 13. I understand that if I participated in certain advanced education programs, I may be required to reimburse the United States government as stated in written agreement made by me with the United States government under law and regulations.
>
> 14. My current duty telephone numbers and email are as follows:
>   Commercial:
>   Email address:
>
>
>
>   NAME
>   RANK, Branch

- SHARP MFR: Memorandum stating whether you were a victim of a sexual assault as defined by the DoD Sexual Harassment/Assault Response Program (SHARP) on unit letterhead. Example:

Office Symbol   DATE

MEMORANDUM FOR RECORD

SUBJECT: Victim of Sexual Assault Statement for Administrative Separation

1. DOD Instruction 6459.02 and AR 600-20, chapter 8, Sexual Assault Prevention and Response Program Procedures requires Soldiers being administratively separated to sign a statement answering the following questions:

    (a) Did you file an unrestricted report of a sexual assault in which you were a victim within the past 24 months: **YES**   **NO**

    (b) If the answer to (a above) is YES, do you believe that this separation action is a direct or indirect result of your sexual assault, or your reporting of the sexual assault?
    YES   **NO**   **NA**

2. Point of contact for this action is the undersigned at [PHONE NUMBER].

                                  NAME
                                    RANK, Branch
                                    SSN

- 4187 requesting retirement.

- Retirement award write-up. If you want your packet to move forward, you'll probably write this yourself. I discuss my thoughts on it later in this chapter.

- Leave forms (PTDY and Transition Leave— discussed in this chapter).

S-1 will continually ask you for more paperwork than is on the HRC website. Without that paperwork, the packet isn't leaving your unit, so just grit your teeth and find page three of your original enlistment documents that wasn't uploaded to iPERMS 25 years ago (trust me on that one). If you were ever in the Reserves, ensure you download and print your DA5016, Chronological Statement of Retirement Points, and include that in your packet as any Active Duty time for training or mobilization will count towards your retired pay calculations. Also, if you've ever had a break in service or transferred between components, you'll have a DD214 for any Active Duty time. Give copies of those DD214s to S-1 for inclusion in your packet.

It took about 30 days for my retirement packet to leave my unit. Once it leaves the unit, it goes to Retirement Services, more on that in a later chapter.

Retirement Award

This is where you really need to look hard at yourself in the mirror and ask the person looking back at you if another award really matters. I get it, we all want to be recognized for what we've done. Years of twelve-plus hour days, blood, sweat, and even tears have gone into your career. But what does one more ribbon get you? People at your next civilian job won't care that you got a Legion of Merit versus another Meritorious Service Medal. I know a lot of soldiers who were dead-set on getting that LOM award at retirement, who went through all the hoops with their rater to get the paperwork completed and approved in the correct format, only to have their final DA638 show that their award was downgraded to an MSM somewhere along the chain because it ended up being late anyway.

We've all been around the military a long time, and seen a lot of really poor leadership decisions—don't get me wrong, the vast majority of my experiences have been positive, but go with me here. The retirement award is one last time for a petty senior leader to get their licks in. I was the rater for a Plans Section sergeant major who'd been in the Army for 28 years, pissed off quite a few people because he was confident and a little arrogant because he was very good at his job. I originally submitted him for a LOM and was told flat out by our O-6 that it would be downgraded, so to save the sergeant major the embarrassment, I reworked it and submitted it as an MSM. For almost a year, I asked about his award status and was continually told it was being worked. The day before his retirement ceremony, I was told that they'd downgraded the MSM to an Army Commendation Medal. The sergeant major had never been in any trouble and he was devastated when I told him that he was getting an ARCOM for 28 years of service to our nation. Never underestimate the power of people to hold grudges.

I opted to simply write my award as an MSM. Yes, just like you've probably written most of your own awards and/or evals in the past, your retirement award is no different. In the end, it's just another ribbon that you may or may not even remember what it's for, however, you will remember the final sting of a downgraded award, I promise you that.

Transition Leave

Everyone calls their last period of leave in the Army "Terminal Leave," but the correct term is "Transition Leave." It's what the counselors at SFL-TAP and the Retirement Services personnel use, so it's better that you understand that the terms are synonymous.

Determine how much leave you'll have on the last day of service by looking at your LES and figuring 2.5 days of leave per month. Be sure to account for leave you have already submitted, plan to take, or have taken that has not yet been subtracted from your leave balance. Your company commander can approve up to 60 days of transition leave. Anything more than that and it has to go up to the next higher commander. Make sure you find out how your commanders handle this. In my last unit, the Group Commander normally wouldn't approve any leave beyond the 60 days, and directed soldiers to take leave throughout the year to reduce their balance. In that instance, no amount of arguing that it was your leave and that you should be allowed to take it was heard. Find out early how much your commander will approve so you're not just burning leave your last year.

It's important to note that your transition leave form *must* end one duty day prior to your retirement because you have to return to the installation to Final Out.

Your transition leave form is submitted with your retirement packet. They won't accept your packet without the leave form, so even if you don't know what your plans are yet, you have to submit something. Don't worry; it can be changed later on if you didn't get it right the first time.

Permissive Temporary Duty (PTDY)

Another benefit that you may not be aware of is that you are authorized to take up to 20 days of permissive temporary duty for the purposes of job hunting. This is a benefit, not an entitlement, so your command does not have to approve your request. Pro tip: You can take four 5-day blocks of PTDY during the week and not use it up by including the weekends.

One thing to note that I've mentioned elsewhere in this guide: Your final day of PTDY and transition leave should be separated by two weeks. Otherwise, you'll be required to clear while on transition leave. For me, I took my 20 days of PTDY, then came back for two weeks to clear, then took my 60 days of transition leave, so it was almost like having 3.5 months off.

SFL-TAP

For the Army, one of the first things you have to do in preparation for retirement is to register for the SFL-TAP program. Even though I completely understand the need for a transition assistance program, I still have a love-hate relationship with SFL-TAP. There's a lot of good in the program and a lot of really bad requirements that add on to your already overcrowded plate. Unfortunately, it's a mandatory requirement for anyone leaving the Army, so it's one of those things that you must do in order to get your DD214.

The military is set up for you to succeed. Yes, there are a ton of dummies who screw it up, but for the most part, you will get promoted on a regular schedule, earn more pay as you gain seniority and rank, and will have access to more resources than you know what to do with. Once you retire, that goes away. While you'll still have access to many more benefits and resources than your civilian contemporaries, whether you succeed or fail is one-hundred percent up to you as a civilian. The hand-holding stops and you're pushed out of the nest to either fly, or fall flat on your face. SFL-TAP *can* help to set you up for success.

SFL-TAP is really a two-part program. You have the Army's portion, Soldier for Life (SFL), and the DoD-mandated Transition Assistance Program (TAP). The paperwork requirements of the SFL portion will likely give you fits, whereas the TAP portion is covered by a Department of Labor instructor who goes over a pretty good portion of how to navigate the civilian world after you separate.

Once you've decided on your retirement date, you can begin going to the Army Retirement webpage 18-24 months out to do your initial counseling with SFL-TAP. There's an online portion and an in-person/telephonic interview that are both required. Once those are complete, you can begin accessing the SFL-TAP classes at your installation, even up to 18-24 months out. Very few of the classes are mandatory, and some are quite helpful. For instance, I took the Federal Hiring Process course three times to ensure I got all of the information—which I'll share in the Your Next Career chapter of this guide.

You can enroll in the SFL-TAP workshop once you break the 12-month mark. There's a mandatory 5-day workshop that gives you a little bit of pertinent information for managing your transition. The program is mainly about giving you the tools to go out and dig up the information yourself. You can be assigned to any TAP office you choose—even on sister service installations. This means if you live in the DC area, for example, where there are a lot of installation options, you could enroll at the installation closer to your home. I was told that once you do the mandatory 5-day workshop, you're "stuck" with that office and can't change. As with everything else I've learned with the retirement process, that wasn't true. You can switch back and forth, and I did, depending on what classes were offered where and what was convenient for my schedule.

The 5-day workshop is, well, it's certainly something. Half of it was really bad, half of it was really good. My best advice to you, like a lot of these requirements, is to just do it and get it over with. You'll be in class with a bunch of E4s completing their first enlistment, soldiers who are being chaptered out, soldiers who are at their 10- or 15-year mark who've decided they are completely done with the system, servicemembers from other branches, and a handful of soldiers trying to complete the class requirements so they can retire. In my opinion, SFL-TAP is *not* really set up for retiring soldiers, it's simply a CYA by the DoD to say that they gave every veteran the tools for success after the completion of their service. You will likely not be given the information you need or expect in their standard briefings, so ask the questions and make them come back to you with an answer.

The SFL-TAP workshop is broken down into three main areas. The first is the SFL-TAP specific stuff where you'll start working on your documents required to get cleared by SFL-TAP (Gap Analysis and Individual Transition Plan). During this first part, you'll do a skills crosswalk, which no joke, said I'm qualified to be a short-order cook or a barista, 20+ years of senior staff planning be damned. Just laugh it off and do the requirements. You'll also do your post-separation budget and do a follow-on phone conversation about it. I've got a short chapter in this guide dedicated to finance, so just know that you will do an extremely in-depth budget for SFL-TAP. Keep it and use it!

The second area of the 5-day class is the VA brief. I was most looking forward to this one so I could determine a way ahead...and was the most disappointed in it. The instructor was terrible and didn't know anything about the VA or its processes, but she had great stories about her son who has PTSD from OIF1. It was extremely disheartening that the instructor wasn't able to provide any pertinent information. Thankfully, someone in my class put me in contact with a great VSO who helped me with my VA disability claim, which we'll talk about in the chapter on the VA.

Part three is taught by the Department of Labor and the instructor was a retired Marine. He was a great instructor who tried to impart as much information as he could in the three days we had with him. You'll refine (or start) your resume, work on your interviewing skills, and develop your elevator pitch. In addition to the GAP, ITP, and the budget, you'll be required to submit your resume, and either proof that you've applied to two jobs or have a job offer letter to complete SFL-TAP. This was annoying. If you follow the very rough SFL-TAP schedule of going through the class as early in your process as possible, then applying for a job twelve months out from retirement is wasting your time and the two companies that you apply to. It's a mandatory requirement, so you know the deal: shut up and color.

At the end of the 5-day class, SFL-TAP wants you to schedule your Capstone interview where you turn in all of your SFL paperwork, plus the DD2648 with a counselor. The DD2648 has to be signed by your battalion commander or higher, so plan some time and gentle reminders to them that they need to sign it in the system. Save that DD2648 because you'll have to turn it in at your Final Out appointment.

During the workshop, they'll also ask you to print your Verification of Military Experience and Training (VMET) from the VA website. I found it mildly interesting what was included in this document and what wasn't. The VMET did come in handy when preparing my master federal resume due to all of the school and job-specific verbiage that could be transferred over.

Besides the course, SFL-TAP hosts classes, webinars, and job fairs. I signed up for a lot of classes, including taking one of the classes multiple times to ensure that I had all of the information. The job fairs were critical for me because I hadn't been "job hunting" in over twenty years.

Going through the process, even when I was too far out from retirement to be of any interest to the recruiters, was a valuable experience that helped me land my post-retirement job. Of course, you know I've got a chapter on post-retirement employment, so be sure to check that out if you plan to work after you retire.

RETIREMENT SERVICES

I've told you that one of your first stops needs to be calling or going into your retirement services office. You can begin the retirement process online with the SFL-TAP classes and everything that they offer, but sooner rather than later, you're going to need to figure out where the Retirement Services office is hidden on post. The one at my installation was just that, literally hidden in a derelict building, down a long, depressing corridor and around the corner. Oh, and there were no signs directing the way. Seriously.

Once you find the office, you'll need to get signed up for their pre-retirement briefing, which gave literally the exact same information as the SFL-TAP classes, with the exception of Finance and Transportation. Without the pre-retirement brief, you allegedly can't get your clearing papers when it's time. I'm not sure as to the validity of that statement, but I can easily see them withholding the paperwork because you didn't follow their instructions. At my final installation, the pre-retirement brief is taught once a month and there are only about 20 seats per class. Every office is probably run differently, so take this as an anecdotal experience. To sign up for the briefing, I had to sign a paper calendar and it was filled up for three months, so I was glad that I went there early in my process. The restriction on the number of seats was even further limited because several soldiers in my class brought their spouse and a few people were there for information before they'd even decided to retire. There's absolutely nothing wrong with either of those two things—except when people who are in their window can't get a seat.

When I arrived at Retirement Services, I asked if they had a checklist of all the things I needed to do. They don't, of course, but she did give me the attached information sheet which kind of lays out their side of the process a little bit. Of course, she gave me a rapid-fire list of timelines that were verbally different than what are listed on the sheet. However, the gist is that if everything that needs to be complete is done 90 days prior to the start of your PTDY date then you "should" be good to go. That's partially true, but more on that as we go along.

Fort Meade Retirement Services Office
2234 Huber Rd., Rm 210 & Rm 214
301-677-9434/9600
Hours of Operation: Appointments: 0800-1200   S1 & Walk-ins: 1300-1500

Ready to retire? What should I do to start the retirement process?

If you are thinking about retiring in 12 months or more, your first step should be signing up for your SFL-TAP classes. The SFL-TAP process can be initiated up to 24 months from your requested retirement date. For information on signing up for SFL-TAP classes contact the SFL-TAP office at 301-677-9871. These classes are required for all transitioning Service Members.

What about retirement specific transition classes?

The Fort Meade Retirement Services Office holds the Pre-Retirement Briefing the 2nd Thursday of every month (except December) from 0900-1600. In addition to the SFL-TAP classes, the Pre-Retirement Briefing is also required for all retiring Soldiers (spouses are welcome to attend). You may attend the Pre-Retirement Briefing as many times as you would like both before and after retiring.   Seating is limited so in order to attend the briefing, you must sign up in advance to have a spot reserved. To sign up please stop by the Retirement Services Office or call 301-677-9434/9600. The uniform for the briefing is either your duty uniform or civilian attire. All attendees will be notified of where the Pre-Retirement Briefing will be held in advance of the brief date.

***There is no Pre-Retirement Briefing during the month of December
***You are welcome to attend the Pre-Retirement Briefing prior to submitting your retirement request or making a definite decision to retire. Many Soldiers attend the briefing to gather information to make a more informed decision about when to retire.

What does the Pre-Retirement Briefing consist of?

- Claims (legal)
- Intro to Retirement
- Johns Hopkins (medical coverage options)
- SFL-TAP (brief overview—not SFL-TAP classes)
- Public Health Command (post-retirement health and fitness)
- Survivor Benefit Plan (SBP)
- TRICARE
- Finance
- Education Center
- Transportation
- KACC Medical Records

How do I submit my retirement request?

Every Soldier (Enlisted and Officer) must go through their S-1 first to submit their retirement request. The S-1 is responsible for turning in the retirement request to the Fort Meade Retirement Services Office no more than 12 months from the requested retirement date and no less than 9 months from the requested retirement date. If the request is submitted less than 9 months from the requested date, the packet must have an exception to policy memo. The S-1 is responsible for turning in all packets and picking up all retirement orders. Soldiers are not to turn in their own packets as it is an S-1 function.

What documents does a retirement request packet consist of?

- DA Form 4187 requesting retirement—must be signed by O-6 (Enlisted)
- Memo requesting retirement (Officer)
- O-6 endorsement memo-O-5 and below or GO endorsement memo-O-6 and above (Officer)
- Initial enlistment contract (pages 4/1, 4/2, 4/3 only **DD Form 1966 can replace 4/3)
- Initial oath of office (Officer)
- Prior DD Form 214/NGB 22 or any prior discharge documents (if applicable)
- Retirement point sheet (if applicable)
- DD Form 93 (updated within one year)
- SGLI (updated within one year)
- Sexual Assault Statement Memo
- DA Form 31 (PTDY & Transition)
- ERB/ORB (current within 30 days)
- SFL-TAP Requirements Met Form (Provided by SFL-TAP office upon request)

What happens once my retirement request is submitted to my S-1?

Once your packet is submitted to your S-1 it will go through the required review process IAW your unit SOP until the packet is ready for submission to the Retirement Services Office.

What happens once my retirement request is submitted to the Retirement Services Office?

When the Retirement Services Office receives your retirement request packet it will go through the review process to verify that the packet meets all requirements for retirement. Once that has been done, the necessary information will be updated in our system to generate the DA Form 2339 for enlisted Soldiers or the DA Form 7301-R for Officers. You may be contacted directly by the Retirement Services Office with information pertaining to your packet. You will be given the opportunity to review your retirement application (DA Form 2339 or DA Form 7301-R) prior to submission to HRC. Officers are not required to sign the DA Form 7301-R, but enlisted Soldiers are required to sign their DA Form 2339 in order for the request to go forward to HRC. The Retirement Services Office services all of Fort Meade and any Soldier requesting to use the Fort Meade RSO as their Transition Center. HRC has the entire Army to service. Please keep this in mind in terms of processing times. With all the proper documentation your packet will be submitted to HRC in approximately one week. Once your packet goes to HRC the processing time is approximately 3 weeks. Every individual request is different, so processing times may be shorter or longer depending on what HRC finds when they're reviewing your retirement request.

What happens when my retirement is approved? Disapproved?

When the Retirement Services Office receives notification of your retirement approval, we will move forward with finalizing your retirement orders and provide a copy to your S-1.

If your retirement request is disapproved, the Retirement Services Office will notify you and your S-1 of the status and the reason for disapproval. Disapprovals can happen for various reasons. Please feel free to contact the RSO directly for information on options moving forward.

What happens once I have my retirement orders?

When you have an approved retirement and you have received your orders, the remaining steps are as follows:

∞ Schedule your one-on-one Survivor Benefit Plan (SBP) counseling at least 60 days prior to the start of your PTDY. **Please keep in mind that if you are married and choose any option other than full SBP coverage, your spouse will be required to attend the SBP counseling with you and will have to either concur or not concur with your SBP decision. If your spouse resides in another state you will be advised of how to complete the SBP process during your appointment. YOU WILL NOT RECEIVE YOUR RETIRED PAY IF YOU DO NOT COMPLETE THE ONE-ON-ONE SBP COUNSELING.

∞ Fill out your certificate request form (provided by the RSO). You will receive the following items:
- -U.S. Flag (box also contains Soldier for Life stickers/decal and lapel pin)
- -Tri-Signed Retirement Letter (signed by SMA, Chief of Staff, Secretary of the Army)
- -Certificate of Appreciation signed by the Commander in Chief
- -Retirement Certificate signed by the Chief of Staff
- -Spouse Certificate (if applicable)
- -30 year letter for Soldiers with 30 or more years of Active Federal Service

∞ Fort Meade does not have retirement ceremonies. Outside of any ceremony your unit may provide, it is an option for Retiring Soldiers in the National Capital Region to attend the ceremony conducted at Joint Base Myer-Henderson Hall. To sign up please visit https://www.mdwhome.mdw.army.mil/ceremonial-support/army-retirement-ceremonies

∞ According to the start date on your approved DA Form 31, you will receive your installation clearing papers 10 duty days from the start date of your PTDY. When you receive your installation clearing papers you will also receive a WORKING COPY of your DD Form 214 to review prior to your final-out appointment.

∞ The day you receive your installation clearing papers and WORKING COPY of your DD Form 214 you will take those documents along with your approved DA Form 31's and retirement orders to the Finance Office to schedule your final-out appointment with Finance. Your final-out appointment with the Retirement Services Office will be AFTER you complete your final-out with Finance.

∞ If your PTDY and Transition leave are taken consecutively, your final-out appointment will be on the last duty day prior to the start of your PTDY. If you're taking your PTDY in increments prior to starting your Transition leave, IAW AR 600-8-10, you are required to have one duty day between the end of your PTDY and the start of your Transition leave. During that one duty day between the end of your PTDY and the start of your Transition leave is when you will final-out.

∞During your final-out you will review the WORKING COPY of your DD Form 214 and make any updates/corrections prior to finalizing the document. If you have questions or are unclear about anything on your DD Form 214, please ask for clarification prior to signing the final copy. You will need the following documents in order to final-out with the Retirement Services Office:

-Completed unit and installation clearing papers
-DD Form 2648 (signed by you, the SFL-TAP counselor, and your Commander)
-Finance Transition Form

What if I still have questions about the process?

The Retirement Services Office is here to assist you. If you have any questions at all you can always contact our office and we will assist you however we can. Enlisted retirements is covered in AR 635-200 and Officer retirements is covered in AR 600-8-24.

How do I get assistance after I retire?

As a Retired Soldier, retirement services are available to you for life. If you have questions or need assistance with anything post-retirement you can always contact your local Retirement Services Office for assistance.

As you can see, the information that Retirement Services provided is only a small part of the massively jumbled up retirement puzzle. While I was there, I verified that my retirement packet was at HRC. I also wanted to verify with them what they sent forward. Wouldn't you know it, some of my enlisted documentation that I'd given to S-1 (and accounted for almost 5 years' time in service) wasn't in the packet that they sent forward. Luckily, I had a copy of everything with me that I gave them right then and there, otherwise, my retired pay calculations would have been about 12% off. Which reminds me, have a binder with you, along with your calendar. I'll add that to the chapter on Everything Else.

DD214 Worksheet

The most important role of the Retirement Services office—after sending your retirement packet to HRC—is developing the DD214 Worksheet. By now, we all should know that the DD214 is the Certificate of Release or Discharge From Active Duty. The DD214 is the single most important document that you will get from the military upon separation and you'll likely be asked for it as verification for all sorts of reasons. This document includes all periods of service, awards, overseas and combat tours, as well as the character of discharge **for this period of service**. I put that last part of the previous sentence in bold for a reason. If you've transferred between components, say from Active Duty to the Reserves, then back to Active Duty again, then you won't see the dates listed for your other periods of service on your DD214. You will, however, see two blocks that state your total prior Active Duty time and total prior Inactive Duty time. Check those closely. You'll want to have any other DD214's you've received with you in your binder.

Retirement Services will provide you with a DD214 Worksheet after you receive your retirement orders. The DD214 Worksheet looks exactly like your real DD214, with the exception of the word "WORKSHEET" stamped diagonally across the document. Review this form thoroughly. Then do it again. Set it aside and review it again later. I'm not joking. If the worksheet is wrong, your final DD214 will be as well, and it is a nightmare to get your DD214 corrected after you separate. If there's wrong or missing information on the DD214 worksheet, contact Retirement Services immediately to get it corrected.

Survivor Benefit Plan

You won't see the folks from Retirement Services for a while after the pre-retirement brief and either picking up or receiving the emailed copy of your DD214 Worksheet. The next time you do see them will be for the Survivor Benefit Plan (SBP) election. You can make your election no earlier than 60 days prior to the start of your transition leave. The SBP election has to be completed in person. If you decide that you're not going to take it, your spouse is required to come with you and sign the paperwork declining the SBP.

You know that your monthly retirement paychecks cease once you die, right? The SBP is an annuity for your spouse if you die before them. You have to pay a percentage out of your retirement check to "buy" the annuity. If you took the SBP, upon your death, your spouse would receive a portion of your retirement paycheck until his or her death. It's important to note that the annuity they would receive is not your entire retired paycheck. The Retirement Services representative can tell you the exact costs and annuity amount at your SBP election appointment.

There's a ton of information online about the SBP, so I'm not going to color your opinion one way or the other if it's a good or a bad deal. There may be life insurance options that are much cheaper and might pay a higher overall death gratuity. Do your research and make your own decision about SBP and whether it makes sense for your situation.

After SBP election, you're transferred to Transition Assistance office. They'll be who you direct any further questions to. In reality, the next time you see any of them will likely be at your Final Out appointment.

MILITARY MEDICAL

I hate to keep saying that this leg of the Retirement Stool or that leg is the most important part of retirement, but this is probably *the* most important part of your military retirement. If you haven't already begun doing so, begin your medical now!!! Yup, I went there. *Three* exclamation points. It's that important. You can quickly run out of time if you don't begin this process early enough because it takes a few weeks to get appointments and then each successive follow-up is another few weeks.

My last assignment was as a support officer in a special mission unit. The Group physician's assistant was terrible about prescribing medications without putting anything in MEDPROS, and since we had our own aide station, stocked with prescription medications, it was easy for him to do. He actually told me to my face when I asked him about it, that the VA doesn't care about what's in your Active Duty medical records, it's all based on their compensation and pension exam as he gave me medication that absolutely should have been documented in my medical records, but never was. If you've had someone tell you something along those lines, let me be the first to tell you that they are unequivocally wrong. The VA looks to your military medical records to help establish a service connection. My dad always told me to do my own research and to take information presented at face value, regardless of who presented it. In this instance, I wish I'd taken his advice. Make sure that every interaction with a medical professional is annotated in MEDPROS.

There is no going back to get something put in your records after you retire, so spend all the time you can to get this right. You will be glad that you did yourself the favor later on.

Routine Medical

If you're like me, you've probably kept some ailments undercover so you could continue to get good assignments/OERs, etc. I get it, a lot of us have experienced command climates that frowned upon going on sick call, but you are at the point in your career where you have to start looking out for yourself because no one else will.

Here's a quick horror story from my experience with a bad PCM. I was about 18 months out from my chosen retirement date when I decided to see my Primary Care Manager (PCM) about my injuries. I simply couldn't do all the cool-guy physical stuff that my unit engaged in any longer without popping four 800mg Motrin before and the same amount afterward. My liver was going to give out on me. I made an appointment with the actual medical clinic, not the Group PA, since I was fairly confident that he was just giving everyone meds to treat the symptoms, which kept us going on the mission, without treating the causes of the injuries or illnesses. When I arrived at the clinic, my PCM listened to my list of physical issues. Hand on the Bible, before I even finished telling her everything that was bothering me, she said that she wasn't going to address my complaints because I had ailments, many of which were over five and ten years old, that should have been seen long before then. Her statement to me was along the lines of if I'd lived with them that long, then they really must not be that big of an issue. I'm not going to pretend that I said something nice to her, and before I left the medical treatment facility, I had words with her commander, who assigned me to a new PCM. This is your retirement, don't let some doctor or physician's assistant derail your progress. Months later, when I had to do my annual Periodic Health Assessment, my former PCM was stamping off on the questionnaires instead of seeing patients. I'm not sure if that's a punishment or a demotion from seeing patients, but her bedside manner certainly earned her that position.

After I switched PCMs, my new doc began working through my list of problems, scheduling multiple appointments because she could only examine three or four things each time. The time between her evaluations, referrals, X-Rays, and MRIs were easily a couple of weeks for each item, then the specialists' findings took a week, and then I had to add another week to schedule a follow-up appointment to discuss results with my PCM… As you can see, time, or lack thereof, adds up quickly. It's better to start this process as soon as you can so you can spread out your appointments, especially if you have an extremely busy assignment, go TDY a lot for your job, or your command team isn't supportive.

TRICARE Online

Before you request a copy of your medical records, determine what's on the TRICARE Online portal. Go through your personal records and upload any documents that you may have that aren't there, especially any outside referrals and diagnoses as those are notorious for not making it into the system. TRICARE Online: https://www.tricareonline.com/tol2/prelogin/desktopIndex .xhtml.

Also, if you ever served on a joint assignment in the past and were treated at non-Army facilities, those records likely didn't transfer. This problem is supposed to have been fixed by consolidating all medical under the Defense Health Agency. However, I know from personal experience that being treated at Bethesda Naval Medical Center from 2008 to 2013, my treatment records did not transfer over from the Navy system to my Army medical records. See why all those old-timers used to tell you to keep copies of everything?

Medical Records

Once you've gotten all of your medical issues documented in your records and begun treatment, go to your installation's treatment facility or hospital to request a copy of your medical records. They say that it takes about 30 days for all of the files to get burned to a CD because they have to scan all of your paper records and download the digital records. Mine only took a couple of days since there were literally no paper medical records for me. Silly me, I'd allowed the Army to ship them one time when I PCS'd instead of hand-carrying like I usually did…and they got lost. No joke, when they finally tracked them down, I got the folder that everything used to be in and about three pieces of paper. That was all that was left. I was at the nineteen year mark when I discovered that special nugget of information.

The first thing you should do with the medical records CD is to go burn a copy to a spare CD. I even saved all of the files to my laptop at home, just in case. Next, you'll want to spend some time at the copier. When you finally make your initial VA appointment with your Veteran's Service Officer (VSO), they'll require you to bring both a digital copy of your medical records and a printed copy. Yup, all thousand pages of it, or whatever the amount ends up being. Trust me, it takes a long time to print that much paperwork, especially if you're using a shared printer and aren't trying to jam it up while your peers are printing their work.

Be sure to compare the medical records that you get from the hospital with what is available on TRICARE Online. One of the things that I found a discrepancy with was regarding X-Rays and MRIs. My medical records did not contain all of the doctor's notes that my TRICARE Online did, so I pulled that info down from the site and added it to my records that were submitted to the VA.

Retirement Physical

After you have your medical records, call to schedule your retirement physical. This can be done anywhere from four to six months out from your retirement date. You should get a packet emailed to you or handed to you when you schedule the appointment with several different forms. At a minimum, you should get a DD2697, a DD2808, and a DD2807-1. Fill them out completely. Most importantly, make sure you're honest on it. This may be the last time to get something annotated in your records. If it hurts, say so. You'll also have to schedule lab work, a hearing exam, and provide a copy of any active physical profiles you may have.

Make sure you bring the forms that you pre-filled out to your retirement physical. During the exam, tell the provider *everything* that you may be concerned with, even if it is already on the paperwork or if it hasn't been previously annotated. The doctor should give you a thorough exam and then complete their portion of the forms. If you're lucky, they'll do it while you're sitting there and scan it all into the system so you can leave the appointment with the paperwork in hand. This was one of the times that I got lucky. Within a few hours, the physical did show up on TRICARE Online, so you can also download it from there because you'll need a copy of your retirement physical for your VA disability claim, if you file one.

Finally, you may have heard the myth that once you've done your retirement physical, you don't have to do PT anymore. This is simply not true. What *is* a fact is that once you've completed your Army retirement physical, your unit cannot require you to take the APFT/ACFT for record. However, you still have to do normal unit PT. So, if your commander schedules a diagnostic ACFT as part of your daily unit PT, for example, then you'll be required to do it.

This wraps up the Military Medical leg of the Retirement Stool. There wasn't necessarily as much information in this one as some of the other legs of the process, but it is by far the most time-consuming and likely the most important. Start early and spend as much time as you need to in order to get this right. Become very familiar with TRICARE Online and how to navigate that system as well. It'll pay dividends in the long run.

FINANCES

We're going to step aside from the Retirement Stool for a moment to look at another important aspect of your retirement: your finances. My best friend is a financial planner, and he would probably strangle me if I didn't give you at least a little ear worm about finances. While this guide is about the retirement process, it is extremely important that you understand your pre- and post-retirement finances and how the loss of more than 60 percent of your income will affect you and your family. What? More than 60 percent? That's a typo, right? Wrong. We'll discuss the types of retirement and the percentages associated with them shortly. For now, you need to know that your retired pay is based solely on your base pay. That sweet, sweet tax-free Basic Allowance for Housing and the little bit of cash that Big Daddy Army gives you for the Basic Allowance for Subsistence are both gone once you retire. If you were lucky enough to receive Pro-pay (professional pay), then that's gone too. You can only base your military retirement income on that little chart that gets published by Congress each year—and once you're in retirement, on annual Retiree Cost of Living Adjustments (COLA).

I got it, you've got all your ducks in a row and know exactly how things are going to be. Kudos. So did I…then reality hit and I was pulling from savings to make ends meet for that first month and a half after retirement. If at all possible, pay off as much debt as you can before you retire. Doing so will make your income stretch so much further than paying interest on credit cards or installment loans.

Please, give this section a read-through and don't skip over it. There are a few nuggets of advice, some definitions of terms, and, hopefully, some funny little anecdotes hidden in here as well. And, as always, these are just my personal observations and experiences, I am not a financial advisor or planner. If you think you may need professional financial assistance, seek one out to help you with your planning.

Types of Military Retirement

There are three types of retirements (really four, but I'm not going to cover REDUX at all). If you don't know which one you're in, then you have a way bigger problem than trying to drop your retirement paperwork.

The High-36 plan (or High-3 as most people call it), is the more traditional program that people associate with the military retirement system. It equals 2.5% times the number of years of service, times the average of the member's highest 36 months of basic pay. The High-36 is available for soldiers who entered the service after September 8, 1980, but before January 1, 2018.

The newer Blended Retirement System (BRS) is the only retirement plan for members with an initial date of entry into service on or after January 1, 2018. However, it is an optional retirement plan for members with an initial date of entry into service on or before December 31, 2017, who meet certain criteria. Under BRS, all covered members receive a Government contribution that equals 1% of basic or inactive duty pay to the Thrift Savings Plan (TSP), a tax-advantaged retirement account. Additionally, covered members have the ability to receive up to an additional 4% matching contribution from the Government to TSP beginning after 2nd year of service through 26th year of service. Those servicemembers who stick around until retirement based on longevity of service will also receive a defined benefit that is 2.0% times the number of years of service times the member's highest 36 months of basic pay.

Finally, there's the military Disability Retirement. This is different than receiving disability compensation and benefits from the Veteran's Affairs (VA). Disability Retirement is funded by the DoD while the VA's disability compensation is funded by the VA. They're different pots of money, and you can receive both, however, I am absolutely not an expert on how to navigate the two systems in conjunction. Soldiers determined medically unfit for continued service with a DoD disability rating of at least 30% are eligible for this type of retirement. If you find yourself in this retirement category, get smart on it quickly to ensure you don't miss any deadlines.

Retirement Calculator

You should learn all you can about what system you're in and visit the Retirement Calculators section on the MyArmyBenefits webpage. The calculators are invaluable and can help you estimate how much you'll earn in retired pay, as well as allow you to play with adding months and years to your service to determine when is the best time for you to retire. For me, every month extra I served added about thirty bucks, pre-tax, to my retired pay each month, so play around with it to help determine your timeline. Here's where the calculator can be found: https://myarmybenefits.us.army.mil/Benefit-Calculators/Retirement.

What's important to understand about retired pay is that it's based on the pay scale *when you retire*. If you get a pay raise, it's based on the annual cost of living adjustment (COLA) passed by Congress, not on changes to the military pay scale. For example, my father retired as an E-8 in the 1980s and his monthly retired pay is significantly less than an E-8 who retired in 2020 due to the large annual pay raises the military received in the past twenty years or so. The COLA raises weren't nearly as large of a percentage as the military pay received.

Final Pay

I can already see your eyes rolling back in your head. I just went through the different types of plans and their benefits, which is extremely boring. That's one of those things that I felt I needed to show you. Now, on to why you're really reading this section: the money.

As I mentioned in the foreword of this chapter, I struggled during the month and a half following my retirement. What people say versus what is reality is usually different. Your final pay is the last Active Duty paycheck that is held back while the Army performs an audit of your account to determine whether you have any outstanding debts. If you get paid two times a month, the 1st and the 15th, then your paycheck that you normally would have gotten on the 1st will be held since that paycheck covers the second half of the previous month, not the current one.

The finance officer at my final installation told us at the pre-retirement briefing that you *may* have a delay in getting your final pay while the Army performs the audit, but it rarely goes longer than six weeks. And before you ask why you would have a delay when there's a full 12-month retirement process, just shake your head and remember your last twenty years of paperwork always getting messed up. Finance won't even begin their audit until you Final Out of the Army. Score one for government efficiency!

Here's my story. I retired on 31 August. You may have heard that you can only retire on the 1st of the month…that's partially true. You actually retire on the last day of the month and are placed on the retired rolls on the 1st. But I digress. I retired on the 31st. Did my Final Out with finance and all of that (more on the process later), then went home. And waited. And waited. October 1st rolls around, still no final pay. I remembered the finance officer's statement about it could take up to six weeks, so I waited some more. October 15th hits and I call DFAS.

Of course, me, being the smart retiree that I think I am, called the Retired Pay section—the phone numbers can be found on their website and I'll publish them in the Resources chapter at the end of this guide as well. After being on hold for forty-five minutes or so, I finally talk to a human. Only to find out that Final Pay issues are handled by the Active Duty Pay section. Ugh…can you see where this is going?

So, I sat on hold for a long time after getting transferred to the new number, and discover that lo and behold, there was some screw-up at my installation where they didn't properly click a box or dot an "i" or something equally as stupid. The DFAS people couldn't be bothered to correct the issue. It was my responsibility to get in contact with my base finance office and have the problem corrected. Remember, at this point, I've lost my CAC and government computer. Have you ever tried to find a working phone number from a base directory on a public website? I finally get through to the right person after being bounced around a few times and the woman was extremely apologetic and helpful. She did whatever her office was supposed to have done six weeks earlier, then it took about ten more days to make its way through all the wickets before DFAS paid me.

And, to add insult to injury, they'd taken out about $125 for some debt or other that I never bothered to try to figure out because I was just fed up with the process at that point. Long story short: once you decide to retire, begin squirreling away cash to cover your expenses during that lull between your retirement, when you receive your final pay, and when your retired pay kicks in. It will likely be at least six weeks while Finance conducts their audit; it may be longer.

Retired Pay

The good news is that your retired pay is pretty much automatic as long as somebody didn't screw up along the way. Your retired pay is paid the same as your Active Duty paycheck, ie: you get paid in arrears for the previous month. So, for example, if you retire on 31 August, you can expect your first retirement paycheck to arrive on/about 01

October. It's not going to be the gross amount that you calculated in those online retirement calculators, though. The government's gonna get theirs, so you need to know that you will pay federal taxes on your retired pay and possibly state taxes, depending on where you choose to retire.

One other note about the taxes. If you choose to work after you retire (yes, I have a chapter on this too), you will more than likely see an overall pay increase with the combined incomes. I'd never really had to account for "extra" money while serving in the Army, and got hit with a fairly large tax bill the first year of having those dual income streams. Do yourself a favor and have some additional money withheld from your paycheck for federal/state income tax. If you accidentally give too much, you'll get it back when you file and you can adjust your withholding. That's a much better error than having to pay, a lot. Just my two cents.

State Income Tax

Choosing where you want to live when you retire comes down to a lot of different factors. For the purpose of this guide, consider the state income tax, property taxes, and cost of living. If you've been a resident of a state that doesn't have a state income tax for your entire career, suddenly getting hit with a state income tax bill may come as a shock to you.

Here's a great map I found online from the AARP website that gives you a quick glance at how states tax your military retired pay:

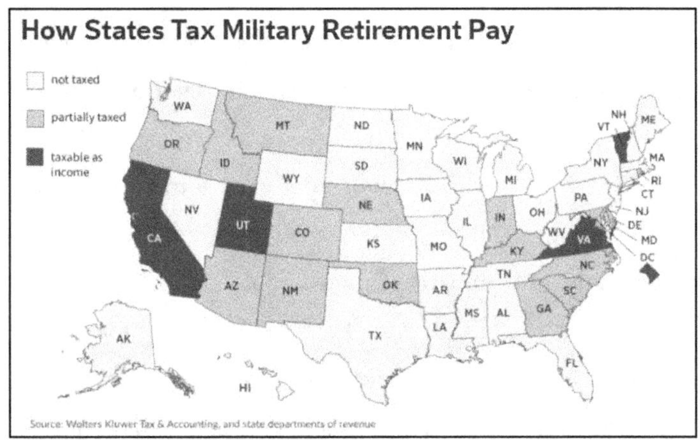

The Military Benefits website gives a more detailed list of the various rules and laws on each states' books, so be sure to check that out here as well: https://militarybenefits.info/states-that-do-dont-tax-military-retirement-pay/

Depending on where you choose to live in the US, it is entirely possible to never have to work a day in your life again, and it doesn't have to be someplace in the middle of nowhere. Your retired pay and benefits are huge, something that the vast majority of the nation's residents will never be eligible for. If you don't want to work, seek out a location where your pay will cover the costs of living and enjoy your retirement.

Where you choose to retire could also be dependent upon the state benefits for veterans with a VA disability rating. Of course, you won't know if you'll be eligible for certain types of VA benefits until after you've already retired, but just know that most states also have additional benefits for our disabled veteran population beyond what is granted federally.

There are a lot of other great resources out there to help you decide on where you want to settle down once you do retire, and laws are always changing, so be sure to do your research about your chosen state if taxes and cost of living are one of your concerns. One thing you can try is to perform a web search with "military.com (State Name) VA State Benefits". The military.com page will open with a brief snapshot of some of the more researched benefits for that particular state and it'll include a link to the actual (state name).gov website which provides more detail in regards to the state you're interested in. What I tell folks is to look at the states, compare the benefits; and if one has better benefits than the other that will allow you to enjoy a better quality of living, and you don't mind living in that state, move there and apply for the benefits. Remember, every state is different, however, most states have a residency requirement in order to claim state benefits.

Thrift Savings Plan (TSP)

The TSP is a tax-advantaged retirement account that the crusty old E-7 at your first unit probably told you about. While I hope that you took advantage of the TSP throughout your career, it may be too late at this point. You cannot continue to contribute to the TSP once you separate.

There are several options available to you with regards to the TSP after you leave the service. You can simply leave it where it is and let the government continue to manage the funds at an extremely low operating cost, you can roll it into a civilian 401k, or you could even take out a TSP loan to help you with certain costs, such as buying a home—although hopefully, you'd use your VA benefit for that!

You should do your own research on the topic. www.tsp.gov is a great resource with a lot of information and helpful calculators. Your retirement accounts are for the long haul, 10, 15, 20 years down the road, and in most cases, you can't withdraw from them until you reach a certain age. My only advice to you is to keep those retirement accounts open, if you can. We've all seen the 84-year old grandma handing out shopping carts at Wal-Mart and wondered if she chose to be there for the interaction with people, or if she had to be there to help pay the bills. Be one of the people who chooses to be there.

Finally, even if you decide to work in the federal government as a second career, your military and civilian TSP accounts will be separate unless you go through the process of combining them. Personally, I like to keep mine separate and compare their growth over time based on different allocation strategies. Some would say that I'm a nerd like that.

Budget

The last section in the Finances chapter is about your budget. You need a rock-solid understanding of how much money you expect to be coming in versus your bills, savings, and potential emergencies that may arise. This is extremely important if you choose not to work after retirement.

I'm not going to give you the crazy list of every contingency that you should prepare for, you'll have the SFL-TAP classes to do that. Yes, you have to prepare a budget as one of the Capstone requirements to complete SFL-TAP. However, I do want you to think about your financial situation and what the implications of losing the guaranteed income are. Retirement from the military, and the complete lack of hand-holding that goes along with it, is both exhilarating and frightening. The more you prepare yourself and your family by laying out realistic expectations, the smoother your transition should go.

Thank you for indulging me on reading through this chapter on finances. If we were to use our Retirement Stool analogy, finances are the duct tape holding those legs on the seat. If your grasp of your finances and how the loss of Active Duty income benefits aren't solid, then everything else could come crashing to the floor. Before you even think about retiring, spend some time doing some serious soul-searching and number crunching to see how things are going to be.

EVERYTHING ELSE

As I've said before, the retirement process isn't linear. There are a lot of little ankle-biter tasks that fit in multiple places—or not anywhere at all. In an effort to capture all of these, I'm going to use this chapter as a "catch all" for the administrative minutiae of the retirement process that are each very important in their own right, but don't necessarily fit in anywhere else.

The order the items are listed in this chapter are in no way indicative of their importance. They're simply listed in alphabetical order for ease of use.

Binder

I mentioned this briefly in the Retirement Services chapter. Having a binder that you bring with you is key. I bought a waterproof one that zipped closed and had an accordion divider inside so I could put paperwork in its respective place. The accordion divider made it very easy to find paperwork quickly. The binder was huge for me as several times I needed paperwork or proof of whatever and luckily I had printed copies of what was needed with me. Otherwise, I would have had to try to reschedule time to return to the office that I'd finally been able to get into.

For convenience, I also kept my retirement notebook in there, along with some pens and my paper calendar.

Calendar

For me, getting a hand-written calendar was extremely important. In the civilian world, I keep everything in my phone, but I worked in a secured compound that didn't allow cell phones. On top of that, I worked inside the SCIF, so there were literally no type of electronic devices allowed for me to keep track of appointments except for my work computer…I didn't have access to my work computer outside of the office. There were a few times before I went with a hand-written calendar that I almost missed a medical appointment because it was either on my cell phone or in my Outlook calendar and I didn't have access to one or the other at the time. Missing an appointment would have set me back further in the process and there's not a lot of time to do things twice.

After I made the switch to a paper calendar, I took it with me everywhere (work, home, and car). Doing so allowed me to make appointments anywhere I was, including inside my work facility, without the dreaded memory dump the moment I left work and hadn't put the appointment into my phone once I got to the car.

If you don't have a printed calendar, get one!

CIF

You know the deal, you certify that your clothing record is correct once a year by going to AKO and looking at what's listed. Then you give a copy to the supply section and you're in compliance with the requirement. The funny thing is, that clothing record online isn't the one that matters. What the Central Issue Facility (CIF) has in their system is the only record that counts. If it's feasible for you to do so, I recommend going out to CIF and having them print a record of what they have in their system. Examine it closely, items marked as a "PCS turn-in" or "ETS turn-in" will need to be returned to the government. In my case, the list online was very different from what CIF expected me to turn in. Luckily, somebody had told me that before, so I brought literally everything I had for turn in—four duffle bags worth of gear.

I enlisted in 1995 and got my initial issue of BDU items in 1996 at Basic Training. They were the woodland camouflage pattern. Then I went through ROTC, got my commission. We were issued DCUs in the desert camouflage pattern when my unit deployed to Iraq. Then we got ACUs and were issued items in the UCP pattern for deployment to Iraq. Next came the OCP pattern ACUs for deployment to Afghanistan. Then came Multicam pattern items for the regular issue. Okay, do you see a *pattern* here?

Sorry, had to fit a dad joke in this guide somewhere. Looks like this was it.

So, I had five different types of uniform patterns and gear. For those of us in the DC region, who aren't in the Old Guard, there's only one CIF around, and it's down at Fort Belvoir, which is almost an hour and a half drive one way. Going down there for their version of the list was a hassle in my opinion. When it came time to turn everything in, I just brought everything I could find.

In the end, CIF wanted a little of each type. I'm not even joking. I don't know what their reasons were for the random items they chose either. For example, CIF wanted my BDU field jacket back. That thing would have been twenty-five years old. Of course, I didn't have it. It's long gone. But, they *were* willing to take my DCU field jacket in lieu of the BDU pattern. Thankfully I had that with me. There were lots of weird, random little things that they wanted, and others that I thought for sure that they'd want that they didn't take (hello, Kevlar underpants still in the plastic wrapping. I'm looking at you). I took four almost full duffle bags of gear with me for my final turn in and brought home more than two bags of stuff. Thankfully, I didn't have to pay anything, because given the commute, that's what I would have done rather than playing the back-and-forth game.

Bottom line, this is just another oddity of the retirement process. There didn't seem to be a reason why they did or didn't want a particular item returned. Go with it. You earned that giant smile on your face when CIF stamps your clearing papers that you've cleared their station.

Clearing Papers

Speaking of clearing papers, you'll get your clearing papers two weeks before your transition leave begins. As mentioned before, ensure your PTDY and transition leave are separated by at least two weeks, otherwise you'll be required to clear during leave or PTDY. Transition services will email these to you, so make sure that you either check your military email account at home (probably a good idea) or that you've provided your civilian email address to them.

Your installation clearing and unit clearing papers are nothing special. It's the same old documents you've seen a dozen times in your career. The only difference in the clearing process is that you'll be turning in much more of your issued gear than you've had to in the past. Otherwise, you're still clearing the post library, dental, medical, etc.

DEERS

This is another one of those no-brainers that you're probably scratching your head wondering why I'm listing this as a topic. Just do me a favor and ensure your dependents are listed properly in DEERS before you retire. If there's one thing I've found, it's that you can actually make relatively easy progress while you're still on Active Duty. Once you're a retiree, take a number, bud.

DoD Ethics Letter

If you're even considering government contracting after retirement, go see your unit/installation JAG. They can prepare a letter of DoD Post-Government Employment Opinion Advice for you. This document covers a whole host of post-government employment restrictions, specifically whether you worked with contracts or certain contracting companies that you may be interested in applying with. This is a federal requirement and every single government contractor that I applied to wanted this document, so go see your legal advisor for proper advice!

Download Your Files Off Your Work Computer

This seems like a no-brainer. Once you retire, you won't have access to anything on your work computer. The real kick in the shins is if you were planning to download everything during those two weeks of clearing between your PTDY and transition leave and the S-6 already swiped your computer to reimage it. Didn't happen to me, but that's what they did to a buddy of mine. There's no getting your files back at that point.

I recommend starting this one early. There are issues with accessing your iPERMS after you no longer have a CAC. When you try to go to the site, it immediately asks for a login certificate associated with your CAC. From iPERMS, download and save everything. I mean *everything*. This is where your evaluations are kept—which are a huge help in writing your resume, your enlistment/commissioning documents, your service school transcripts, your award documentation…literally your entire Army career is on that site, and you should have a copy of everything before you lose access to it.

The same goes for calendars, especially if you're planning to get a Project Management Professionals (PMP) certificate, which wants dates, hours, and descriptions of projects. Having copies of your calendar for the last few years, in conjunction with your evaluations, will help you in getting all of that information together.

DS Logon

This is one of those things that we almost always just select "Logon with CAC" when prompted to enter our DS Logon. Remember, you won't have a valid CAC or a .mil email account after your Final Out appointment, so take the steps to establish a username and password prior to separation. You will be required to have a DS Logon for the VA once you begin that process, as well as accessing TRICARE Online, and several other websites.

There's literally no reason not to do this right now—after you read this guide, of course.

Dual Military

This is one of those things that a lot of soldiers, especially male soldiers, discount. However, according to a 2011 Pew Social Trends report, 48% of military women are married to male servicemembers, while only 7% of males are married to female servicemembers, and those numbers are likely only going to go up as more women choose to serve in our Armed Forces. I was a dual military spouse and I understand just how hard it is to balance two high-performing, high-demand careers. The "good" news is that one of you—whomever is reading this guide—is about to retire. That doesn't mean all of the stresses will go away, especially if you choose to work after retirement, but you may not be worried about both of you going to the field at the same time, both parents being deployed, etc.

If you have children and both of you aren't retiring at the same time, you should begin making the preparations a few months in advance of your retirement. Switch the BAH-with rate to the spouse who's not retiring. Enroll all of your children under the spouse who's staying on Active Duty in

DEERS—to include making sure that the *retiring* servicemember is linked in DEERS to the servicemember.

When you retire, get both your blue retired servicemember ID card and your tan dependent ID card. My recommendation is that you enroll the retiree under the Active Duty spouse in TRICARE so they are seen at the Active Duty dependent priority versus the retiree priority. Just remember when refilling your meds after you retire to put in your Active Duty spouse's DoD ID number!

Government Travel Card

If you have one, don't forget to close your government credit card prior to leaving Active Duty. Depending on your unit and their requirements, you may close this as early as you need to. However, if you plan on using it during the move to your retirement home of record, discuss that with your installation Travel section as there may be rules associated with that type of use after you've retired.

Hiring our Heroes

Hiring our Heroes (HoH) is a Department of Commerce program to put retirees/separating servicemembers into the corporate workforce as interns while still on active duty. It's a recognized SkillBridge program, so as long as the commander allows you to be gone for about three months, this is a huge opportunity.

HoH runs several cohorts a year near the major installations. They fill up quickly, so if you're even remotely interested, contact them early.

https://www.hiringourheroes.org/

MyPay

You will access your retiree pay information through MyPay. You'll need to set up a username and password while you have your CAC, because you won't have a common access card after you retire. The password expires every 150 days, so don't worry about making the perfect one that you'll always remember. Just write it down.

If you're able to do so, set up your post-retirement banking information before you retire. I've said it before and I'll say it a dozen more times throughout this guide, everything is just easier while you're still on Active Duty.

There's a little down arrow at the top of the page labeled "Choose an Account" to toggle between your Separated Army Active Duty account and your Army Military Retiree account. Your LES, Leave and Earnings Statement, that you got on Active Duty is replaced by the Monthly Retiree Account Statement (eRAS). You still have the option to set up allotments, designate beneficiaries, and change banking information from the retiree account side that you had on the Active Duty side.

You cannot contribute to the TSP from your retired pay, so there's no TSP information there. One last thing about MyPay that I mentioned in the Finances chapter is your federal withholding. I got hit with a very large tax bill the first year of my retirement because my civilian income combined with my retired pay was more than I had been making. You can adjust your withholding on MyPay to withhold more taxes each paycheck in an effort to head this off until you have your tax implications figured out after retirement.

Notebook

I recommend getting a notebook that is solely dedicated to your retirement process. It may seem annoying to have two notebooks, your daily military one and your retirement notebook, but it will help you stay organized instead of flipping through your daily book trying to find the page that you scribbled those notes on.

Also, as an aside, I recently, finally, went through my old paperwork and had a nice little bonfire—I kept paper copies of everything I actually needed, don't worry! I had twenty years' worth of training certificates, forms, old CIF records, fifteen copies of every set of PCS travel orders, and probably ten old green notebooks with information from previous units that I always thought I might need later on. Yeah, all that went up in flames. I didn't need to worry about accidentally burning important retirement information in one of my green books because I'd kept all of that in my retirement notebook.

Post-9/11 GI Bill

If you choose to transfer your Post-9/11 GI Bill to your dependents, ensure that you make your elections before you separate! Whether that's to your spouse or children is obviously up to you. As of this writing, there is discussion about allowing servicemembers to transfer benefits after they separate, however, it's not gone beyond the discussion phase in Congress. Do it the easy way and request a transfer before you separate. You may be able to change the number of months allocated to a dependent after you retire, but as with everything, it will likely be harder after you've done so. I elected to transfer just one month of eligibility to my youngest child while splitting the rest with the other two so that all three were associated under me. If the other two don't use it, I can roll those months down to the youngest one.

Print Copies

I know it's 202X and printing copies of documents is old school. However, you will absolutely need a printed copy of your medical records to submit to the VA if you file for a disability claim and there will certainly be times when you may need a paper copy of items, like your leave forms or retirement orders once you get them. Having paper copies will help you out in the long run—ensure that you also have everything digital and send them to your civilian email address as a backup.

Professional Certificates

I'm not going to spend a whole lot of time on this topic, but know that your SFL-TAP office can put you in contact with your state's Department of Labor offices to assist you with obtaining professional certificates. For example, the Maryland DoL stated that if there is a certificate of any type, they can help get you enrolled in the required course at no cost to you and will either pay for or assist with the cost of certification testing. It's a very good benefit that's worth exploring if you have a professional certificate of some type in mind.

Retirement Flag and Certificate

As a retiree, you are entitled to one folded American flag, a Soldier For Life lapel pin, and a retirement certificate signed by the President of the United States. This is supposed to be automatic and will be given to you at your retirement ceremony or by your unit when you depart there for the last time. However, if your S-1 shop isn't on their game, or the installation Transition Services office is slow, you could be left high and dry. I've seen it happen where soldiers did not receive their flag and certificate prior to signing out and driving away from the installation. The promise that "it's in the mail" is never a very good one.

Check in periodically with your S-1 a few months before you retire to ensure they've received your items and have them on-hand to present to you.

Selling Back Your Leave

This is one of those things that people either swear by or hate the idea of. You can sell back a total of 60 days of leave during your entire career. It does not matter if you had a break in service, it's a *total* of 60 days, ever. If you opt to sell back some leave, you'll be paid only your base pay. BAH, BAS, and pro-pay aren't included in the pay for selling your leave. It's paid as a lump sum, which is taxed at a flat 25% rate.

Conversely, those who are opposed to selling back leave say that you should take all of your leave, get paid your normal pay during leave, and begin your next career while earning double pay. I can certainly see the merits of this as well, but there may be some extenuating circumstances that would make selling your leave more preferable to you.

First, if you get started on the retirement process late, you may simply not have time to take the leave, so of course, it would make sense to sell it back. Secondly, as in my case, your commander may not approve any leave you have beyond the 60 days of transition leave that you are entitled to by regulation. Third, maybe you really need some extra cash and are willing to accept the higher tax rate in order to get the money.

There is a whole host of reasons why one way or the other may be better for you. The only sure thing I can tell you is that your leave balance will be exactly zero on your first day of retirement, so figure out what you need to do to ensure that you don't lose any of it. I've included the link to a military.com webpage about this topic in the Resources section to help you determine what's best for your situation.

Statement of Service

I'm only going to briefly mention this here since this chapter covers actions that you need to do while still on Active Duty. I cover requesting a statement of service in depth, with an example, in the Your Next Career chapter. If you plan on working in the federal service or government contracting, and are applying to jobs before you retire, you'll need a statement of service signed by your commander. Obviously, this has to be done while you still have a commander! It's just another step along the way and something that I'll add to the checklist at the end of the guide.

Transportation

One last thing on choosing where you retire: the military will move you one final time *after* you retire. Yes, you read that correctly. The government will move your household goods one final time to a destination of your choosing after you retire. I'm sure there a ton of fun rules associated with it, so you can read all about it on www.move.mil.

You have one year to use this benefit, however, it can be extended for a total of five years by calling or emailing your installation travel section annually. I'll post the link in the Resources section.

TSP

While I cover the Thrift Savings Plan in the Finances chapter, it's important to note that the TSP won't be withdrawn during your final month in the Army, so you'll see the extra money in your final pay check.

If financially possible, you may want to adjust your TSP contribution to allow you to get the most money into this tax-advantaged program. Of course, that's a lot easier to do if you're retiring in, say, November instead of March.

VGLI

Veterans' Group Life Insurance (VGLI) is a life insurance policy available to retirees. You will be covered by the SGLI for 120 days after separation. After that, you will not have life insurance if you haven't made other arrangements. VGLI may be competitive with some other policies available on the market, so I recommend that you do some research to see what works best for you. Be careful not to sign up for a policy that has low premiums at first, and then quickly escalates as you get older. A lot of retirees find themselves sort of "stuck" with a bad policy because by the time they realize the premiums have become unaffordable, the cost to get a new policy is cost-prohibitive.

You must enroll in VGLI within one year of retirement. Don't worry, the VA will send you emails reminding you. All. The. Time.

FINAL OUT APPOINTMENT

Your Final Out appointment is actually fairly anti-climactic as far as I'm concerned. You've spent all this time and effort going through the military medical process, sat through way more SFL-TAP classes than most people feel are necessary, and you've gone back and forth with the Retirement Services and Transition Services personnel. This is it. This is the day you've waited for!

You'll have your appointment with Transition Services. They'll look at your unit and installation clearing papers, your SFL-TAP Capstone documentation, and verify your leave form. That's it.

Next, you'll have a meeting, either face-to-face or telephonic, with Finance to go over their estimates of your final pay. As mentioned in the Finances chapter, don't expect to receive your final pay for a while due to the audit that DFAS performs on your account. Six weeks is average, mine took about seven and a half due to clerical errors at my installation.

After Finance, you're done. You are free to go forth and do great things. You've sacrificed a lot for this moment. Enjoy it, but don't do anything dumb like getting blitzed and getting in a car accident on your way home from the retirement celebration. You owe it to yourself and your family to earn your retired paycheck for the next fifty or sixty years.

AFTER SEPARATION

You've made it. The air smells sweeter. The grass actually *is* greener. Heck, you get to sleep in past 0430 because you don't have to be at PT every day. Enjoy your retirement. You earned it.

Like I've said throughout this guide, things aren't in lock-step order, so while you could complete certain aspects of your VA claim while still on Active Duty, I listed it after the other chapters on purpose. However, there are a few other items that you need to follow up with the military once you've retired; things that couldn't be completed while still on Active Duty. I've placed those in this chapter.

ID Card

Your retired Identification Card is one of those items that Retirement Services said you could do "a few days before you retire." They were wrong. The folks at the DEERS/RAPIDS section won't see you to issue that shiny new blue retired soldier ID card until you're fully retired, with your final DD214 in hand. Also, be aware that they run on an appointment system, so be smart and schedule this a few weeks *before* you retire.

As mentioned in the Everything Else chapter, ensure you get your DEERS straightened up before you retire. This will make everything run so much smoother for you at the

ID Card office. And don't forget to get your dependent ID card too if you're dual military.

TRICARE Insurance Coverage After Separation

You've had TRICARE for the past 20+ years and you're just going from one duty status to another. It should just transfer right over with it, right? Wrong. You'll be dropped by TRICARE on Day 1 of your retirement. Even better, we were told in our retirement briefing that they won't let you switch from the Active Duty coverage to retiree until after you retire (this is wrong as you'll see in the next paragraph). In my case, I listened to the TRICARE briefer's advice and called during that first week of retirement. I got signed up for the coverage, but there was a 30-day lapse in coverage due to their rules. I was fortunate that nothing happened to me during that time.

Of course, I found out during my many conversations with the current contracted TRICARE representative that the miscue on my part could have been avoided before I retired. You *must* elect your retirement benefits desired by the 20th of the month prior to your retirement or you and your family will lose one month of benefits immediately following retirement and won't be able to receive care. So, for example, if you're retiring on 01 March, you will need to enroll into your elected benefits by 20 January (remember the whole confusion between "retiring" and being "placed on the retired rolls"?) to ensure that your medical insurance coverage doesn't lapse.

To enroll, simply call TRICARE at 1-877- TRICARE and state that you are retiring and want to make your benefit changes accordingly. Currently the cost for TRICARE's family plan is right around $540ish per year and the Co-Pay is 12 bucks.

Retiree Recall

Yay! You've made it to retirement and will never have to put on a uniform again. Well, maybe yes and maybe no. Debbie Downer time. Enlisted members are transferred to the IRR until they reach a total of 30 years of service, and are then fully retired. Officers, however, have no such rule and can be involuntarily recalled to service at any time after they retire. While this is rare, it can happen. Remember when General Schoomaker was retired, golfing or whatever, at the start of OIF? He was recalled to Active Duty to be the Army Chief of Staff.

One other thing to note is that retirees remain subject to the UCMJ. Don't do anything illegal and you're gonna be just fine.

https://www.military.com/join-military/eligibility-requirements/can-you-really-be-recalled-active-duty-any-time.html

Take Care Of Yourself!

In this last section of the chapter, I want to address something extremely important. You need to take care of yourself. How many times have you heard that one of the soldiers that you knew, or at least knew of, dropped dead of a heart attack just a few years after they retired? For me personally, it's been a lot. Probably more than twenty. I simply can't fathom going through an entire career, sacrificing your body and your time, to simply fall out after the finish.

My doc, the one who would help me, not that other lady, told me that one of the main causes for this is heart disease brought about by very treatable and manageable hypertension—high blood pressure. Ensure that you're going to the doctor regularly. Hell, you can even buy an over-the-counter blood pressure monitor online and check your BP regularly. Hypertension is usually defined as a blood pressure over 140/90. If either of those numbers are higher than that, it's time to see a doctor.

In addition to keeping track of your medical needs, you still need to get some exercise. I get it, a lot of folks swear they are never running again after they've spent the last twenty running almost every day. Leading a sedentary lifestyle after retirement will kill you. You don't have to run or do push-ups and sit-ups for exercise anymore if you don't want to. Go for a walk to start your days, or go in the evening after meals. Join a gym. Take up tennis or pickleball. Go swimming. Buy a bicycle (please, for the love of God, do not ride on two-lane back country roads!). Anything that gets you moving and elevates your heart rate for thirty minutes or more a day is a very good thing.

Also, if you choose not to work after retiring from the military, or even if you do, get a hobby if you don't already have one. Pick something that will help you to relax and spend a few hours a week doing it. Treat that R&R time like an appointment on your calendar and commit to yourself.

Bottom line: If you give up on yourself, how will you take care of those who need you most? Take care of yourself. You've spent 20+ years of your life defending our nation. Spend the next 50 years enjoying your life.

DEPARTMENT OF VETERAN'S AFFAIRS

The Department of Veterans Affairs (VA) is the fourth disjointed leg of our Retirement Stool. It's a separate government agency and has its own processes that are vastly different from the DoD activities that I've described so far. However, your VA disability claim and VA healthcare after retirement are dependent upon your time in the Army. It is paramount that any and all of your chronic ailments be documented by the VA, and hopefully designated as a service-connected issue. A physical or mental problem that may seem like a minor inconvenience to the forty-something retiree can become a much bigger issue later in life. Like everything else, getting the process started while on Active Duty is a lot faster and easier than if you try to begin after you separate—just know that it won't be completed until many months after you retire. We'll discuss that later.

In this chapter, I'm going to discuss the steps to submit a VA disability compensation and pension claim, the Benefits Delivery at Discharge (BDD) process, your Compensation & Pension Exam, how the VA figures their disability ratings, the importance of a VSO, and a few other items that will hopefully help to demystify the VA for you. I'll also give you a lot of web resources where you can go and learn about the VA benefits yourself.

The VA is probably even more confusing to the new user than the DoD was to an 18-year old at Basic Combat Training. I'm probably only going to hit the wavetops of ten percent of what the agency offers. There simply isn't enough room to cover it all in this small guide. I will, however, share a totally kick-ass list of benefits that a Reddit user put together for veterans later on in this chapter.

VSO—Your First Step

Your VA claim is one of those things that you do not want to do on your own. In addition to the ridiculous amount of forms and requirements associated with the VA, they have a completely different agency language than what we're used to. You may think you're submitting a claim for one thing, but in reality it's something different in the eyes of the VA. To put it bluntly, as one of my friends described it, you *will* get messed over by the VA if you try to do it yourself.

There are many "first steps" during the retirement process. With regards to the VA, I recommend that your first step should be to find a Veterans Services Officer, or VSO. A VSO is a specially-trained representative who can help you translate your ailments into VA language for your claim. They operate free of charge to you and are available from a variety of organizations, including your state's

Veterans' Affairs office, the VFW, AMVETS, American Legion, etc. I've even included a special section later in this chapter for those of you with legitimate SOCOM experience. There are also paid options to have civilian doctors write up your claim, but a good VSO should be able to help you submit the claim the traditional route before you pay thousands of dollars to a third party doctor—especially since there is no guarantee that the VA will grant you a rating. There's a section on the VA.gov website where they maintain a list of approved VSOs who they recognize and will work with.

Horror story time. Okay, not really, maybe more like illustrative example time. A friend of mine retired a few months before me, Special Forces guy, purple heart, all that. He broke his back during an SF jump several years ago. He went through the VA process and all of his issues combined totaled 100% permanent & totally disabled. He got the golden ticket, right? Sort of. The VA denied his service connected claim for back problems. Can you imagine how that conversation must have gone at the VA? He filed an appeal because it was obviously service-connected and there's no telling what could develop as a result of that injury later in life. All of that is to say, get a VSO to help you with your claim!

BDD

In order to get the VA Benefits Delivery at Discharge (BDD), you *must* submit your claim 90-180 days out from your retirement date. While the BDD doesn't actually speed up your processing time, it does enable you to get benefits from day 1 of your separation from Active Duty.

However, the BDD does not mean you begin getting paid on day 1. For me, the failure to tell soldiers that during the retirement briefings was one of the most disappointing things about the SFL-TAP and Retirement Services experience. They made it seem like you begin getting your money right away, which is not the case. The BDD means that if you're found to be eligible for VA disability compensation, then your eligibility for payments will be backdated to day 1 of your separation. That's a major distinction, especially as I've discussed earlier that your Final Pay is six-plus weeks delayed as well.

The VA will take your BDD claim anywhere between 90-180 days out from retirement. This allegedly puts your claim into a higher priority for processing than those who get out, then submit a claim later in life. In reality, what it does is it gets your claim in the VA system. They will do whatever background work is required and contact you *after* your separation to go through the Compensation & Pension Exam (C&P Exam). We were told at the retirement briefings that the C&P Exam happened before you left

Active Duty, but in my experience, the VA did nothing until after I actually retired, then the claim began moving forward.

Your VA Claim

The VA uses the 38 CFR Book C to assist them with their disability rating determination. The 38 CFR lists all of the major body systems and tells you the requirements or level of loss needed in order to be rated for certain issues. I recommend getting familiar with this document as it pertains to your injuries.

In order to find how the VA rates for Mental Health issues, click on the Mental Health tab at the top of the 38 CFR page and then click on the tab that states "Schedule of Ratings – Mental Disorders" once it redirects you. You can do this for every issue you have. You just need to know the body system it's associated with. Once you click on the system, find the Schedule of Ratings, and then start looking through for your specific issue. If you have any issues finding it, please reach out and utilize your local Care Coalition advocate and they will also have the information.

Below is an example chart you can use to help you get started in the process. You should learn how the VA determines ratings and estimate what your potential ratings may be for each ailment so you know, generally, what to expect later on. This can help you with your budget estimates after retirement.

Condition #	Rating	% disabled	Symptoms Write what your symptoms are	DBQ Find the DBQ that applies	38 CFR insert 38 CFR verbiage that applies to condition
			VA Claim Working List		
1					
2					
3					
4					
5					
6					
7					
8					
9					
10					
11					
12					
13					
14					
15					
16					
17					
Overall Rating					

The reason why you need to Service Connect every issue that you have ever had while on Active Duty is that they may turn into health issues later in life. Please don't consider any issue too small. Remember a 0% Service Connected Disability is still a Service Connected Disability that may benefit you in the future as long as it is documented.

Once you've educated yourself on the VA claims process, the 38 CFR, the VA Schedule of Ratings, etc. take the Excel worksheet to your VSO. This will help you remember all of your issues. I recommend bringing it with you to your C&P Exam as well.

What to bring to your meeting with your VSO:

- DD214 Worksheet (or DD214 if you've already separated).
- All previous DD214 documents.
- Printed medical records.
- Printed retirement physical.
- Worksheet with all of your ailments.
- Any medical paperwork that somehow still isn't in the system.
- Bank account routing information.
- Marriage certificate and divorce decrees (if applicable).
- Birth certificates of children.
- Records that indicate you are the primary care giver for adult dependents (if applicable).

Your VSO will walk through all of your ailments with you. This is not the time to be embarrassed about any of your issues. The VSO is not a medical provider, however, what they input into their system is what the VA will see. The doctor at your C&P Exam will only examine the areas that are in the claim, so tell the VSO everything. The VA is notorious for fighting with claimants for years after they submit follow-up claims (seriously, you can get lost down the rabbit hole of reading these horror stories on Reddit boards like r/Veterans). Do yourself a favor and try to get everything possible listed in your initial claim.

C&P Exams

Once you've separated from the military, you should get a call from the VA or a contract company on their behalf. For example, in the DC region, they use QTC Medical, and I never spoke to an actual VA civilian doctor. Don't be surprised if the contracted medical company doesn't call you after that first interaction and everything else is done via text or email. Be on the lookout for emails in your spam folder. Your initial appointment for the VA will be your Compensation & Pension Exam (C&P Exam). This comprehensive exam is the most important exam you will take for the VA…unless you have follow up appointments with a specialist.

A couple of weeks prior to your C&P Exam, you'll receive a packet in the mail of forms called a Disability Benefits Questionnaire (simply called DBQs) that ask specifically about your claimed contentions. Yes, you read that right, you'll get a letter via snail mail. You need to completely fill out these forms prior to your C&P Exam. At first glance, each form looks like something the doctor is supposed to fill out, however, they are for <u>you</u> to fill out. Be sure to do so.

On the day of your C&P Exam, make sure you bring your DBQs with you to the facility for your examination. My exam was in a random office building outside of DC where the contracted provider had their offices, not at a VA medical facility—or *any* medical facility for that matter. That was a little bit of a surprise to me, so, you're welcome. Now you know what to expect. The first thing you'll do after you turn in your paperwork is provide a urine sample. Then, depending on what your claims are, you may or may not need to have blood work done. I was concerned about having a needle inserted into my vein in a sketchy office building, but I haven't contracted an exotic disease from the experience...yet.

When it comes time for the doctor to examine you, they will use the DBQ forms that you filled out. The information you provide is all they'll ask about, so be thorough. You need to ensure that you accurately articulate to the doctor performing the examination the level of loss as described in the 38 CFR. It is often up to the doctor's discretion if a service member provides information that "sort of" sounds like a higher disability to rate at the higher level. If you don't provide all of the information needed, then the same doc has the discretion to rate at the lower rating.

Take your Excel spreadsheet or notes that you need with you in order to help you remember all of your symptoms for discussing with the doctor. Be sure to include things like the amount of time that you miss work because of each ailment, and how it affects your family and social life. Remember the big three Family/Work/Social. An accurate depiction of the extent of your injuries is not a lie or cheating the system. It's you detailing your level of loss for a Service Connected injury/illness/wound/issue/etc.

Remember to articulate based off the 38 CFR Book C rating schedule. Don't be the tough guy that pushed through pain to complete an examination. Especially when the doctor informs you to cease the movement when you feel pain. If possible—and truthful—you should tell the doctor that your injuries are combat related. Start each exam by saying, "While training for combat" or, "During a combat simulation exercise/jump/mission" or even better, "While in combat" that you injured x/y/z.

The C&P Exam focuses a lot on range of movement for musculoskeletal injuries. For example, if you have a bad knee, part of the exam may be for you to bend your knee until you feel pain and then the doc will take this device to measure the angle at which you were able to bend your knee. That plastic angle measuring device is super scientific, you just wouldn't understand.

And that's it, folks. Unless you have a skeletal issue, then they may send you for X-Rays. I had several issues that did not show up on X-Rays, that did show significant soft tissue injuries on MRIs that I had done while on Active

Duty. I figured that since the VA requested X-Rays, they would also want the MRIs that, you know, actually showed the damage, but nope. The X-Rays were good enough and I was able to receive my rating based off of them.

It's extremely important to note that you cannot miss any appointments. If you do so, the VA can stop processing your claim and you may have to start over from the beginning. I also read during my studies that you can only request to reschedule an exam one time before you're labeled as someone unwilling to complete the medical portion and you have to start all over again. I'm not sure as to the validity of that last comment, so play it safe and attend all scheduled appointments or call and reschedule for a time that you know you'll be able to attend.

Your Rating

First off, let me tell you that after your C&P Exam, you'll likely be checking your claim on the VA.gov website every day. It will drive you insane that there aren't any updates and that little disclaimer at the bottom of your claim saying how long until your claim should be complete will make you pull your hair out. I've talked with a lot of people about this: that completion date is almost never correct.

In my experience, when you call the number listed on the website to talk to a representative about your claim, they know less than zero about it. Sure, they can verify that it's actually in the system and tell you whether you went to your exam or not, but that's about it. Talking to a human is almost more frustrating than watching the computer screen.

One day you will finally (FINALLY!) see that the VA has provided an update or a decision on your claim. And their update is that they sent you a letter. G*dd@mm$t!! It's enough to drive you completely crazy. The VA uses the US Postal System for all correspondence. Not email. Not text. Not phone. Mail.

You can wait for the letter, or you can attempt to short-circuit the system. Over on the eBenifits.VA.gov website, you might be able to see the decision prior to the mail arriving, or, you know, getting lost because the USPS is really good at doing that. Once you use your DS Logon to get into eBenefits, click on your Dashboard button. On a desktop it's in the upper right corner. Once on your Dashboard, look for the Disabilities link under the section labeled "Things You Can Do Here". That's where I was able to see what my rating was and what the VA determined to be service connected prior to receiving the letter in the mail.

In addition to what they've deemed as either service connected or not service connected, you'll see an assigned rating for each ailment. You may also see a couple of other statuses, such as STR or Deferred. STR is short for Service

Treatment Record, which is a further examination of your military medical records to determine if you ever sought medical help while in the military for that issue. Deferred means that you will likely be required to go through another exam, this time with a specialist. For my follow-up appointment, I received a text from QTC, the contracted medical provider, telling me where to be and what date/time. I went to the appointment and everything worked out fine in the end.

The VA uses fuzzy math to get to their disability ratings. 20% for one rating plus 30% for another does not equal 50%. It equals 44%, which rounds to 40% for compensation—and consequently does not make you eligible to receive Concurrent Retirement and Disability Pay (CRDP), which is the best option you can receive. I'll discuss the payment options in the following section.

Here's a portion of the VA's Combined Ratings Table that shows how their math works. The link can be found in the Resources section at the end of this guide:

Table I-Combined Ratings Table
[10 combined with 10 is 19]

	10	20	30	40	50	60	70	80	90
19	27	35	43	51	60	68	76	84	92
20	28	36	44	52	60	68	76	84	92
21	29	37	45	53	61	68	76	84	92
22	30	38	45	53	61	69	77	84	92
23	31	38	46	54	62	69	77	85	92
24	32	39	47	54	62	70	77	85	92
25	33	40	48	55	63	70	78	85	93
26	33	41	48	56	63	70	78	85	93
27	34	42	49	56	64	71	78	85	93
28	35	42	50	57	64	71	78	86	93
29	36	43	50	57	65	72	79	86	93
30	37	44	51	58	65	72	79	86	93
31	38	45	52	59	66	72	79	86	93
32	39	46	52	59	66	73	80	86	93
33	40	46	53	60	67	73	80	87	93
34	41	47	54	60	67	74	80	87	93
35	42	48	55	61	68	74	81	87	94
36	42	49	55	62	68	74	81	87	94
37	43	50	56	62	69	75	81	87	94
38	44	50	57	63	69	75	81	88	94
39	45	51	57	63	70	76	82	88	94
	46	52	58			76	82	88	
		53					82		

Special info for soldiers who deployed with SOCOM

Okay, we all know that every time you go into a bar, there are forty-three former SEALs, twelve former SF dudes, and every other person is a Ranger. Don't fake this. If you didn't deploy with SOCOM, the VA will figure it out pretty damn quick. However, if you *did* actually deploy with SOCOM, there is a special statement that may help you establish the validity of your claim. Since I worked as a support guy for an SF Group, I got this information from them, however, I wasn't able to use it myself so all I can tell you is that if the shoe fits for you, read this short section and contact the USSOCOM rep.

Historically, lack of access to records for servicemembers assigned to USSOCOM has prevented the VA's examiners from completely reviewing the submitted claim. This resulted in many claims being wrongly denied. The VA liaison currently assigned to USSOCOM (as of 2021) is Mr. Noel Hike. He can be found in the VA email directory.

The information received from USSOCOM will often be from a casualty report and may be limited to the date of injury, location where the injury occurred, and a brief description of the injury or illness. In some instances, the response will only confirm that the Veteran participated in Special Operations due to the operation still being considered classified.

SOCOM Statement: "I was deployed in support of USSOCOM during multiple times in my military career. The locations, training, missions, personnel and dates remain at a high level of security classification that prevents me from providing specific details. However, utilizing the VA liaison stationed at USSOCOM Warrior Care Program's headquarters will provide any examiner verification of my service, deployments, and other pertinent information for consideration in reviewing my disability rating or service connection."

Special Operations are operations that have the characteristics of combat; therefore, 38 CFR 3.304(d) will apply in all cases where a Veteran's participation in Special Operations is verified.

Alright, we've discussed the claims process, now let's look at a few other benefits and programs available from the VA. When you retire, you'll receive a letter from the VA welcoming you. Inside that packet will be several pamphlets with information about programs offered by the VA. Let me just say, "Wow." No wonder they're always in the news for being super inefficient. They have their hands in all sorts of programs. Not only healthcare, but education, home loans, career counseling, dental care, job searches…the list goes on and on. The VA programs can be extremely helpful if you know where to look, so spend some time looking!

VA Disability Payments

We've discussed the BDD program and how your eligibility for benefits should go back to the first day of your retirement. That's true, however *payments* for your disability, if you are entitled to them, do not go all the way back to the first day. In fact, that first month is treated differently and you aren't paid for the first month that you are out of the service. It's probably easier to just use an example.

By the time you get your rating, you will probably have several months' worth of disability back payments due to you. Remember, the VA, like the DoD, pays one month in arrears. So, let's use our hypothetical retirement date of 31 August and you've received an XX% disability rating from the VA. The entire month of September is not counted for the purposes of compensation—but you are eligible for other VA benefits for that month. The VA disability payment for the month of October is paid on 01 November, the disability payment for the month of November is paid on 01 December, and so on.

Knowing that you don't get paid for the first month after you retire would have saved me a lot of headaches, since I appealed the payment received after I got my first disability paycheck. Of course, it took a while since everything had to be mailed in, but I finally got the answer that I described above. You don't get paid for your first month of eligibility.

Dual Military

It's your benefit, you earned it. I say that because that is what my VSO told me when I asked about how the VA handles dual military couples with regard to compensation. In the Army, only one spouse could claim the dependents and receive BAH at the With Dependents rate. That's not the case with the VA. If you both have a rating of 30% or more, you may both claim your spouse *and* minor children/adult dependents, however the VA does state that it may take them longer to process.

The argument against this is the same as those who argue that dual military should not both receive BAH. Why should they both get the benefit? The answer is: Why shouldn't they? Remember that stat about 48% of women being married to another servicemember? That comes into play here as well. Why should we discriminate against someone for whom they chose to marry? It's their benefit, they earned it.

https://benefits.va.gov/COMPENSATION/docs/bas-dependency-faq-final-508.pdf

10-49% VA Disability

Any disability rating given to you by the VA is a blessing, however, there is more than just a difference in monetary compensation when it comes to how your disability pay combines with your retired pay. You will always be entitled to your retired pay. As mentioned in the Finances chapter, your retired pay is still state and federally taxed as income. VA disability compensation is non-taxable income. Remember, the VA always only works in 10% increments, so you technically cannot be given a rating of 49% as the title of this rule implies.

If you are given a VA disability rating of anywhere from 10-49% then the amount of VA disability compensation is reduced from your retired pay. You'll receive whatever VA disability compensation that you're entitled to from the VA, tax free, and the remainder of your retired pay is still taxable income. So, using simple math, if your retired pay was normally $2,000 a month and you are awarded $1,000 a month in VA disability compensation, then you will receive $1,000 tax free from the VA and $1,000 in taxable income from the DoD.

50-100% VA Disability

A rating in this range is the proverbial golden ticket, and being granted a 100% permanent and total VA disability rating is like winning the keys to the chocolate factory at the end of the movie. If you are rated 50% or above, then you are automatically enrolled in CRDP, which stands for Concurrent Retirement and Disability Pay. That word "concurrent" is huge. CRDP means that you get your full retirement pay, which is still taxable income, but you also receive your VA disability compensation tax free.

So, in our earlier hypothetical example of a $2,000 retired pay, and a $1,000 VA disability compensation, you'd now be entitled to $3,000 a month, with only the retired pay portion being taxable.

While there's not a lot of separation in the amount compensation at the 10-50% ratings, it begins to really add up the higher your VA disability rating is determined to be, and there is a major jump between being rated at 90% and being rated at 100%. Do an internet search of "202X VA Disability Rates" and read through the charts for your current year to see the potential compensation rates. Yes, you get more if you're married, or have additional dependents. Just play around with the charts below to see all of your potential compensation rates.

10% – 20% (No Dependents)	
Percentage	Rate
10%	$144.14
20%	$284.93

30% – 60% Without Children				
Dependent Status	30%	40%	50%	60%
Veteran Alone	$441.35	$635.77	$905.04	$1,146.39
Veteran with Spouse Only	$493.35	$705.77	$992.04	$1,251.39
Veteran with Spouse & One Parent	$535.35	$761.77	$1,062.04	$1,335.39
Veteran with Spouse and Two Parents	$577.35	$817.77	$1,132.04	$1,419.39
Veteran with One Parent	$483.35	$691.77	$975.04	$1,230.39
Veteran with Two Parents	$525.35	$747.77	$1,045.04	$1,314.39
Additional for A/A spouse (see footnote b)	$48.00	$64.00	$81.00	$96.00

70% – 100% Without Children				
Dependent Status	70%	80%	90%	100%
Veteran Alone	$1,444.71	$1,679.35	$1,887.18	$3,146.42
Veteran with Spouse Only	$1,566.71	$1,819.35	$2,044.18	$3,321.85
Veteran with Spouse and One Parent	$1,664.71	$1,931.35	$2,170.18	$3,462.64
Veteran with Spouse and Two Parents	$1,762.71	$2,043.45	$2,296.18	$3,603.43
Veteran with One Parent	$1,542.71	$1,791.35	$2,013.18	$3,287.21
Veteran with Two Parents	$1,640.71	$1,903.35	$2,139.18	$3,428.00
Additional for A/A spouse (see footnote b)	$113.00	$129.00	$145.00	$160.89

30% – 60% With Children				
Dependent Status	30%	40%	50%	60%
Veteran with 1 child only (no spouse or parents)	$476.35	$681.77	$963.04	$1,216.39
With 1 child and spouse (no parents)	$532.35	$756.77	$1,056.04	$1,328.39
With 1 child, spouse and 1 parent	$574.35	$812.77	$1,126.04	$1,412.39
With 1 child, spouse, and 2 parents	$616.35	$868.77	$1,196.04	$1,496.39
With 1 child and 1 parent (no spouse)	$518.35	$737.77	$1,033.04	$1,300.39
With 1 child and 2 parents (no spouse)	$560.35	$793.77	$1,103.04	$1,384.39
Each additional child under age 18	$26.00	$34.00	$43.00	$52.00
Add. child over 18 in a qualifying school program	$84.00	$112.00	$140.00	$168.00
Spouse receiving Aid and Attendance	$48.00	$64.00	$81.00	$96.00

70% – 100% With Children				
Dependent Status	70%	80%	90%	100%
Veteran with 1 child only (no spouse or parents)	$1,526.71	$1,772.35	$1,992.18	$3,263.74
With 1 child and spouse (no parents)	$1,656.71	$1,922.35	$2,160.18	$3,450.32
With 1 child, spouse and 1 parent	$1,754.71	$2,034.35	$2,286.18	$3,591.11
With 1 child, spouse, and 2 parents	$1,852.71	$2,146.35	$2,412.18	$3,731.90
With 1 child and 1 parent (no spouse)	$1,624.71	$1,884.35	$2,118.18	$3,404.53
With 1 child and 2 parents (no spouse)	$1,722.71	$1,996.35	$2,244.18	$3,545.32
Each additional child under age 18	$61.00	$69.00	$78.00	$87.17
Add. child over 18 in a qualifying school program	$197.00	$225.00	$253.00	$281.57
Spouse receiving Aid and Attendance	$113.00	$129.00	$145.00	$160.89

CRSC

If you find yourself under the 50% VA disability mark, contact DFAS and apply for CRSC, if you're eligible. Combat Related Special Compensation (CRSC) gives Disabled Veterans that qualify the opportunity to receive some, if not all, of their DoD retirement money that was subtracted by VA disability money. While CRDP is automatic, CRSC is not, you have to apply for it.

To qualify for CRSC, you must be officially retired from the military. This includes a 20-year retirement, a medical retirement (a disability rating of 30% or higher), retirements based on the Temporary Early Retirement Act (TERA), and Temporary Disabled Retirement List (TDRL) retirees. Additionally, you must:

- have a 10% or higher VA Disability Rating,

- have your DoD payments reduced by your VA payments,
- provide documentary evidence that your injury was incurred in combat (qualifies for a Purple Heart) or in combat-related activities, like war simulation training (practice alerts, war games, live fire weapons practice, hand-to-hand combat training, etc.), hazardous duty (flying, parachuting, demolition duty, etc.), or caused by an instrumentality of war (a vehicle or device used in war, like Agent Orange or weapons), and
- submit an application for CRSC utilizing a DD2860 along with the documentary evidence mentioned above.

Disability Rating Protections

The VA can, and does, periodically review claims and audits what they're paying veterans' benefits for. I've read all sorts of horror stories on Reddit about vets just living their lives, then suddenly their VA disability benefits stop being paid or are reduced. This is because the VA has deemed the injury to have improved over time...often without a medical reevaluation. There are some rules that help the veteran out with regards to this practice.

The 5-Year Rule states that the VA can't reduce a veteran's disability that's been in place for five years, unless the condition improved over time on a sustained basis. The veteran will likely need to present medical evidence to prove that there hasn't been an improvement of their condition.

The 10-Year Rule says that the VA cannot eliminate a service connection that's been in place for ten years or more. However, they can reduce the rating if they have medical evidence that the medical condition improves. There's an exception to this rule if the VA finds out that the original disability rating was based on fraud.

The 20-Year Rule is for a service-connected VA disability that's been continuously rated at or above a certain rating percentage for 20 years or more. The VA is prohibited from reducing the rating below that level. Like the 10-Year Rule, the only exception is if the VA discovers that the rating was based on fraud.

The 55-Year Rule protects veterans from rating reductions if they are over the age of 55. Again, the fraud caveat still applies.

Finally, there is the Permanent and Total (P&T) disability rating. If a veteran is rated 100% P&T, then the VA has determined that their injuries are permanent, meaning they'll never improve over time, and that the rating is 100%. The P&T determination means that the veteran's disability rating will never be reduced and they aren't subject to periodic reevaluations because their conditions cannot improve. As with all of the rules, if the veteran committed fraud during their claim or examination, then it invalidates the P&T protection.

TDIU

I'm only going to touch on this very briefly. The Total Disability Individual Unemployability (TDIU) is a designation for veterans who cannot work due to their disabilities. A veteran is entitled to be paid at the 100% disability rating if he or she can establish that their service connected disabilities preclude them from maintaining gainful employment.

It's a common misunderstanding that a veteran can only qualify for a TDIU rating if they exceed certain percentage disability requirements such as a single service-connected disability rating of 60%, or a combined service-connected disability rating of 70%. The truth is that a veteran can qualify for a TDIU rating any time one or more of their service connected disabilities prevents them from obtaining gainful employment, regardless of the percentage of the disability rating.

There's a separate process for requesting TDIU and information can be found by conducting an internet search for the term. Remember that cases of fraud can invalidate all of your hard work establishing your VA disability rating up to this point, so the TDIU should only be sought out if the individual is truly unemployable due to their disabilities.

Compiled List of VA Benefits

One Reddit user has spent a considerable amount of time compiling a list of all the VA benefits you are entitle to at the various VA disability ratings (they're different), as well as some educational info, and a link to the individual states' pages. I recommend you become familiar with this info.

Here's the goods:

https://www.reddit.com/r/VeteransBenefits/wiki/combinedbenefits?utm_source=share&utm_medium=ios_app&utm_name=iossmf

VA Home Loan

The VA Home Loan program is possibly one of the most recognizable, or at least widely used, benefits. If you've ever purchased a home, then you've probably been asked whether you qualify for a VA loan, even while you were still on Active Duty. The VA isn't a bank, but they will guarantee a mortgage, so there is less risk for a lender, which is why lenders "like" to use the VA Home Loan program. Of course, they also like the fact that you'll likely finance more since you don't have to pay as large of a down payment as a traditional borrower.

You've probably heard of this benefit, and maybe you've even used it. Did you realize that the VA charges a VA Funding Fee for each loan they guarantee? You might not have noticed it rolled into all of the costs during your closing. The VA charges a fee to guarantee your loan. The fee can be paid up front or rolled into the loan and varies by whether it's your first time using the benefit and how much you put down. For example, in 2021, the VA Funding Fee for a first-time use with less than 5% down payment on a home is 2.3%, whereas if you're using the benefit a subsequent time, there's a 3.6% funding fee. The rate drops to 1.65% if you're putting down 5% and 1.4% if you're putting down 10%.

Now, here's something that you might not have known: The VA waves the VA Funding Fee if you have a VA disability rating of 10% or more. That's huge. There is also a possibility of submitting for a refund of the funding fee if you become disabled the same year that you purchased a home.

VA Healthcare

As a retiree, you're entitled to healthcare at military facilities if you continued your TRICARE coverage, and do not need to go to the VA for healthcare. However, there may be reasons why you'd want to, proximity being the number one reason I can think of. Look at what you'd be seeking health care for and decide if you'd be better off seeking treatment with the military or with the VA. That's your decision and what is correct for one person, probably isn't right for someone else.

If you choose to enroll in the VA healthcare system, it's an easy online enrollment. Just go to the following website, read through the eligibility questions and then click "Apply for Benefits" about halfway down the page. You should get a decision within 10 business days about coverage. https://www.va.gov/health-care/eligibility/

Yellow Ribbon Program

This program is huge for those of us who plan to go back to school or who have dependents whom we've transferred our Post 9/11 GI Bill benefits to. The Yellow Ribbon Program can help you pay for higher out-of-state, private school, or graduate school tuition that the Post-9/11 GI Bill doesn't cover. You read that right. If your school participates in the VA's Yellow Ribbon Program and you're accepted to the program, they will help offset the costs of tuition and room and board.

Not all schools participate, but a surprisingly large number of public universities do. The amount of assistance provided also varies drastically from school to school. For example, some schools only accept a few students a year and cover up to a couple thousand in expenses annually, or some schools may only cover undergraduate or graduate programs, whereas other schools accept everyone who's eligible and cover all costs that the Post-9/11 GI Bill does not cover (hello, Florida State!).

The VA Yellow Ribbon program is a game changer for helping pay for college at a public university. Here's the link where you can go in and determine if your chosen school participates: https://www.va.gov/education/about-gi-bill-benefits/post-9-11/yellow-ribbon-program/

eBenefits

This website allows you to do "everything" within the VA system—or at least between eBenefits and the VA.gov websites, you'll be able to do everything. On eBenefits, you'll be able to see where your claim is, start a new claim, upload information requested from the rating party, look at your VA medical records, find resources you may need, and it also has a link to the National Resource Directory, which as its name implies, is a national directory of resources for benefits. If you need scholarship info for kids, search "Scholarships for Military Children/Dependents" in the NRD and it'll populate a list. NRD is a phenomenal resource literally at your fingertips through access in Ebenefits.

Sign up online while you still have a Common Access Card. It will force you to create a DS Logon which will allow

you to access the system using a user name and password.
https://www.ebenefits.va.gov/ebenefits/homepage

Burn Pit Registry

Signing up for the VA's Burn Pit Registry won't guarantee that any of your issues are Service Connected. It will place you into the registry and will provide all of the updates the VA pushes out for educational purposes as to what they are automatically Service Connecting or what they are currently considering. This is the VA's attempt to stop another Agent Orange issue from coming to the forefront of Veteran Health issues.

https://veteran.mobilehealth.va.gov/AHBurnPitRegistry/

YOUR NEXT CAREER

I'm only going to talk briefly here about working after you retire. That is an individual decision and as I mentioned in the Finances chapter, depending on where you live, you might be able to live comfortably on just your retired pay. There are plenty of places where your retired pay will cover all of the cost of living expenses.

For those of you who do choose to work, I highly recommend going through the SFL-TAP courses on the subject. At my installation, the two main flavors of course were entrepreneurship and federal service. That makes complete sense in the DC area, where supporting the federal government is one of the main employment opportunities. There's also government contracting (your active security clearance is worth a lot to employers), state government jobs, civilian careers, teaching...the list could go on forever, so in an attempt to narrow this chapter to my experience, I'm only going to briefly discuss federal contracting and focus more on the federal civilian hiring process. For information about whether you can or cannot work for the federal government while on transition leave, check out the US code 5534a. BLUF: yes you can work as a federal civilian while on transition leave, however, there may be restrictions.

Out of an abundance of caution, I'm going to tell you something that you should already know. Do not put anything classified on your resume! It doesn't matter how long ago it was or what type of agency you're applying to, do not put anything classified on your resume. Besides the fact that it's illegal, there's a practical reason for this. If you're applying for a job at the CIA, do you think they'd be more impressed by what you did downrange or the fact that you could describe what you did in general, non-classified ways that keeps the information secret? Yeah, no brainer.

Elevator pitch

So, you may or may not have heard of an elevator pitch. What that means is a rehearsed, thirty second to one minute "commercial" about yourself that you can give to a recruiter or hiring manager as a way to generate interest in you, your accomplishments, and your future goals. Rest assured, if they're interested in you or what you highlighted in your elevator pitch, they'll ask for additional details. This comes in extremely handy at those job fairs that the SFL-TAP folks always host on the installation.

Be sure to get rid of military jargon and make it so a civilian can understand. For an example, here's my elevator pitch:

"Hi, I'm Brian Parker. Nice to meet you. I'm transitioning careers after 25 years in the US Army. I've spent the last 13 of those years as an organizational design specialist, managing resources at a wide range of organizations from the small functional team all the way up to the corporate level.

As an OD officer, I've helped to ensure that the actions our organizations take today set us up for success 10-15 years down the road. I'm looking for opportunities to leverage the knowledge that I already possess with an organization that's willing to grant me the opportunities to develop additional skills in the future."

When you're first practicing your elevator pitch, it feels kind of greasy, like you're a used car salesman or something. That's essentially what you are, though. A recruiter sees hundreds of applicants a day. You've got to sell yourself and get enough information out there quickly so they can decide if they want to hear any more from you or if they're looking at the person standing behind you in line. Get your elevator pitch right and rehearse it enough that it doesn't sound like you're reading a memorized script.

Federal Contracting

By this point in your career, you know that there is a lot of money to be earned by being a federal contractor. Like, a stupid amount, especially if you stay in the DC area. Headhunters for the companies are everywhere, and if you have a cyber background, you really, really should check out contracting. Companies are literally throwing cash at soldiers with cyber experience. Every single company that I talked with asked about my cyber history (which is pretty much non-existent). That isn't to say that being a contractor isn't for everyone else, though. That's not the case at all. I was recruited based on my abilities to translate civilian requirements into "Army speak" and vice versa. The leadership experience that you've had in the military makes you an ideal candidate for this type of job.

If you are thinking about contracting, remember to get that ethics letter, the DoD Post-Government Employment Opinion Advice, from your installation JAG before you retire. Companies are required by federal law to ensure that you are/were not involved in the work they are doing for the government for a certain period of time.

There are a ton of headhunting companies out there that you can sign up with, or register your resume online at several websites, such as ClearanceJobs.com. I'll put a few contracting-specific websites in the Resources section to help get you started. One resource that you may want to check out is the Federal Business Opportunities (www.FBO.gov). FBO posts all the newly-accepted contracts, so you can set up alerts, find out which company just won a contract in your field of expertise and apply to them while the iron is hot and they need subs to fill the contract.

Federal Civilian Career

Alright, you're ready to begin looking into the civilian world for career options. One thing before we go forward, how the heck do you translate what you've done in the military into a resume and how do you even know what civilian career series to begin looking for?

I've got a couple of resources for you. The first, how to translate your military jargon into civilian language, is huge. The military speaks its own language, something that the vast majority of the population simply doesn't understand. Things that you may take for granted, or even think are a civilian term that the military uses, really aren't. For example, I thought a *1-n* list was a civilian thing. As I described my experiences to potential employers, I always got a blank stare. When I researched it, it is almost exclusively a military phrase for a list ranked in priority from number one all the way to the last item. So, you may need help in writing up that translation. I've placed a website in the Resources section to help you out with this.

As to what civilian career series to look for, this one can be challenging. However, like everything these days, there's a website to help you figure it out. The Maryland

State Government has a website that helps you translate your MOS into potential civilian career series. While it's operated by Maryland, the information is for the entire federal government. This was a huge help to me trying to figure out what skills and competencies that I possessed as a combat arms officer which could translate over into the federal workforce. Here's the site: https://www.dllr.state.md.us/mil2fedjobs/. This website is a lot more helpful than the one SFL-TAP pushes that told me I was qualified to be a barista.

Resume – Federal versus Civilian

We all should know that the standard resume is no more than two pages, with some companies only wanting one page. Typically, they only want to know what you've been doing for the past 5-10 years, your education, a professional summary, that sort of stuff. You should absolutely have that two pager ready to go long before you retire and there are a million sites online to discuss formats and what to include. However, the federal resume is another beast entirely.

The federal hiring process is very convoluted. Your first step should be to develop your master federal resume. The master federal resume can be as long as you need it to be. Mine ended up being 18 pages. The idea behind the master resume is to collect up all of your skills, experiences, and education into one document that you can later pick and choose from as you apply to jobs. To build mine, I used my old evaluation reports, my VMET (Verification of Military Experience and Training) that you have to provide for SFL-TAP, award write-ups, and good old memory—which often seems to fail me. I put every dang thing on there that I thought could potentially be pertinent. Once I was done, I looked at the document and thought, "What a mess." It's a good thing that nobody except you will ever see your master federal resume.

I will admit when I first learned about the master resume in an SFL-TAP class, the instructor wasn't exactly clear and I thought he meant we'd be applying to jobs with the master resume. No, that's not the case. You use the master resume to help you craft your focused resumes. If it sounds like a lot of work, it is. A few days or weeks of work up front is incredibly beneficial down the road, and once it's done, you'll never have to do it again, except to update it with new information.

The beauty of that master document is that you have everything you've ever done to pick and choose from. Read through the job descriptions that you're applying for, then take your master federal resume and trim it down to a rock-solid 4-5 page resume that you'll use to apply to jobs with. Every federal position has different KSAs—Knowledge, Skills, Abilities—that the hiring manager is seeking. Hitting those KSAs is one of the easiest ways to help make it past the first round of cuts. Remember, each position has hundreds, sometimes thousands of applicants, so it is imperative to make it past that first round.

I've heard of people doing some straight up BS things like copy/pasting the KSAs into their resume, shrinking the font all the way down and making it white so it would get recognized by a computer program, but not by a person looking at the document. Don't be that guy or gal. Take the time and adjust your resume to the job posting. You're just wasting everyone's time if you apply for jobs that you're not qualified for. And believe me, you'll likely end up applying for a lot of jobs in order to find one that sticks. It's a lot of work, but well worth it, in my opinion.

Regardless of which type of resume(s) you develop, ensure you proofread it multiple times, double check your contact information, and if possible, have someone else read through it for you to get a second pair of eyes on your work.

Statement of Service

I briefly mentioned this in an earlier chapter. You will need to have the statement of service signed by your commander prior to retirement if you plan to begin applying for jobs with the federal workforce or as a government contractor before you have your DD214. For the federal workforce, your statement of service has to be signed and dated **NO MORE** than four months, exactly 160 days, from the date of your retirement. Mine was something like 172 days and I got several email notices from positions that I'd applied for that I was outside the limits. So, I had to go back on base and get my commander to sign another document, which just wasted everyone's time if I'd known about the strict 160-day limit.

As always, your statement of service should be on unit letterhead. Here's an example of what your statement of service should include:

<table>
<tr><td>Office Symbol</td><td>Date</td></tr>
</table>

MEMORANDUM FOR Whom it May Concern

SUBJECT: Statement of Service for <u>Rank and Name</u>

1. <u>Rank and name</u> is currently an active duty US Army soldier, stationed at <u>installation and state</u>. He will retire with ___ years of active duty service.

2. Date of entry into military service: <u>Date</u>

3. Date of anticipated retirement/separation: <u>Date</u>

4. Character of Service: Honorable

5. POC for this memorandum is <u>Name, contact information (both military and civilian</u>.

<u>COMMANDER'S NAME</u>
<u>RANK, BRANCH</u>

Commanding

USAJobs, ClearanceJobs, and Individual Websites

There are tons of job-seeking websites. For the purpose of this chapter, I'm primarily looking at working within the federal government, either as an employee or a contractor. The main websites for these two roles are USAJobs and ClearanceJobs, with a handful of other, helpful individual websites.

If you want to be a federal civilian, you almost certainly will have to apply through USAJobs.gov, the exception being the Central Intelligence Agency, which has it's own hiring process. There may be a few other one-offs, but the CIA is the big one that I know about from applying there. USAJobs is fairly strait forward, you can pre-load your documents (DD214—or DD214 worksheet—statement of service, transcripts, etc.) and set up saved searches for your area of expertise and salary requirements. I even uploaded my master federal resume and made it searchable so if a hiring manager happened to be scanning for a skill I had, they could discover my resume, however, I never got any hits off of that. You aren't allowed to begin applying to jobs until you're four months out from your retirement date, otherwise, the hiring manager can just deny your application.

Rest assured that you will likely apply to a lot of jobs, several that may be the exact same thing you did in the military, and you won't ever hear back from half of them. I applied to over 120 listings in the four months leading up to my retirement. I was referred (got past the first round) for twenty-nine of them, and only got two interviews. Thankfully, one of those interviews was good and I got the job—I completely bombed the other one and I knew it after I ended the Zoom call. Oh well.

All of that is to illustrate how difficult it is to make it through the government's hiring process. I'm not bragging, but I've had several different directors in my civilian agency tell me that they wished I'd applied to their vacancy before the one I was hired for. The crazy thing is that I *did* apply for those vacancies and never heard anything back from them due to the nature of the process. It's maddeningly frustrating, just don't give up if you want to work for the government after you retire. Persistence will pay off.

There are several message boards on Reddit, such as r/USAJobs, r/FedNews, and r/Veterans, with information about the federal hiring process and they can be a wealth of information. Remember, just as everything you read on the internet, there can be some very good advice and there can be bad advice. It's up to you to take the initial bit of information that you find out and do your own research to determine its validity.

ClearanceJobs.com is a CIVILIAN website that is primarily used by government contractors seeking candidates who possess active security clearances. It costs a lot of money for a company to get a clearance for their employees, so those who possess an active clearance are at an advantage. Just like I mentioned at the beginning of this chapter, do not input anything classified. Number one, it's on an unsecured network; number two, it's a civilian website. Don't get hemmed up because you wanted to try to impress people with all the cool stuff you've done.

Individual company websites are also a great place to seek government contracting jobs. Many of them allow you to set up a profile and perform a "quick apply" once you're in the system. You'll likely still have to search for positions, however, that quick apply capability is a game-changer when applying to twenty different jobs.

There are also websites like LinkedIn, Monster, Indeed, etc. that cater to candidates seeking a federal position. Recruiters do go to those websites and look for qualified candidates, but it is much harder for them to find anyone from the thousands upon thousands of applicants.

Special Hiring Authorities

As a veteran, you're eligible for special hiring authorities. These may be as simple as a veteran's preference or as "special" as a military spouse preference. Most federal agencies have a mandate of how many veterans they are required to employ. Some, like DHS for example, tend to hire many more veterans than other agencies. A special hiring authority does not guarantee a veteran a job, however, it may be the difference between you making it past the first round of cuts or not. In the end, it is still up to you to do well in your interview and to sell yourself appropriately.

Veterans Recruitment Authority (VRA)

This is the "5% Veterans Preference" that you may have heard of. While the VRA allows your application to rise to the top of the pile, it won't guarantee that it will move past the initial cut. It still takes the strength of your resume to keep your application moving forward. You can be appointed under this authority at any grade level up to and including a GS-11 or equivalent. This is an excepted service appointment and upon satisfactory completion of two years of substantially continuous service, you will be converted to the competitive service. There are several requirements that make a candidate eligible for VRA. If you:

- Served during a war or are in receipt of a campaign badge for service in a campaign or expedition; OR

- are a disabled veteran, OR

- are in receipt of an Armed Forces Service Medal (includes the Global War on Terrorism Service Medal) for participation in a military operation, OR

- are a recently separated veteran (within 3 years of discharge), AND

- separated under honorable conditions (this means an honorable or general discharge).

30% or More Disabled Veteran

The 30% or More Disabled Veteran authority allows an agency to non-competitively appoint any veteran with a 30% or more service-connected disability. This is the "10-Point Veteran's Preference" that will allow your resume to make it past the first Human Resources cut and at least be looked at by the hiring manager. There is no grade level restriction for this type of authority.

This authority can be used to make temporary (at least 60 days, not to exceed 1 year) or term (1-to-4 years) appointments in the competitive service. There is no requirement that you be converted to a permanent position, but an agency has the authority to convert such a position to a permanent position if it chooses to do so. You are eligible if you:

- retired from active military service with a service-connected disability rating of 30% or more; OR

- have a rating by the Department of Veterans Affairs showing a compensable service-connected disability of 30% or more.

Once you receive your VA Disability Letter, you'll have to complete an SF-15 and upload that in the USAJobs system to be eligible for the 30% or More Disabled Veteran preference.

Veterans Employment Opportunities Act of 1998, as amended (VEOA)

The Veterans Employment Opportunities Act of 1998, as amended (VEOA) gives preference-eligible veterans the opportunity to compete for positions announced under an agency's merit promotion procedures. It applies only when the agency is filling a permanent, competitive service position and has decided to solicit candidates from outside its own workforce. It allows eligible veterans to apply to announcements that would otherwise only be open to current competitive service employees and certain prior employees who have earned competitive status. Announcements must state VEOA is applicable and as a VEOA eligible candidate, you aren't subject to geographic area of consideration limitations.

To be eligible to be considered for a VEOA appointment, your latest discharge must be issued under honorable conditions, AND you must be either:

- a preference eligible (defined in title 5 U.S.C. 2108(3)), OR

- a veteran who substantially completed 3 or more years of active service under honorable conditions.

Military Spouse Preference

If you are the spouse of an Active Duty military member, you are eligible to be hired under the Military Spouse Preference (MSP). MSP is a special federal hiring authority that allows spouses to be noncompetitively considered for federal positions. Military spouses can identify themselves for MSP through the application process on USAJobs. This is especially useful for spouses who know where they are PCSing to, but aren't physically in the area yet. As long as the position offers MSP (a green icon with wedding rings indicates an eligible position), you may apply.

Spouses can apply for as many jobs as they want using MSP. However, if a spouse declines a job offer extended through MSP, they can no longer use MSP at that duty station.

Buying Back Your Military Time

You might have heard that you can buy back your military time to reduce the amount of time you have to work in the federal civilian workforce in order to be eligible for civilian retirement. It's a great option for non-retirees, and a terrible one if you're receiving military retired pay. In order to buy back your time, you have to give up your retired pay since the government won't pay you twice for the same period of work. That's a bad deal on any day, especially considering the civilian retirement plan is not nearly as lucrative as the military plan—for High-36 at least.

Now, if you got out of the military prior to retirement, and therefore are receiving no payments from the DoD, then this might be a good deal for you. There are calculators on the DFAS site (link in the Resources chapter) that allow you to estimate what your cost would be. Oh, that's right, the term "buying back your military time" means that you're actually *buying* back the time you spent on Active Duty in the military to allow you to reach the thirty year retirement mark sooner since you've already served a part of your time working for the military. It can be a significant cost, depending on the amount of time you want to buy back, and it must be done within three years of beginning your federal career or the cost begins to increase due to interest fees.

Civilian Leave Accrual

As a new federal civilian, you get four hours of annual leave per pay period, after three years in the government, you are entitled to six hours of annual leave per pay period, and after fifteen years, you get eight hours per pay period.

You may be eligible to get credit for your prior military time in order to "jump" up a leave category and there are some important leave accrual options for you. One of them is an entitlement, meaning you earned it and are given the right by government regulation, and the other is a hiring incentive, so it is not guaranteed, however you should absolutely ask for it.

The HR personnel at your new job will know about the standard program of Creditable Service for Leave Accrual where you fill out an SF813 and send it to your military branch's Human Resources Command. The program allows you to get credit for time spent on deployments outside of the US. It shifts your leave accrual start date earlier to account for those deployments and can rapidly push you into the six-hour annual leave accrual category. You request it after you EOD (Enter on Duty) while you're inprocessing.

However, an incentive program than a lot of HR personnel do not know about is the Creditable Service for Annual Leave Accrual for Non-Federal Work Experience and Experience in the Uniformed Service. This incentive allows your agency to grant you credit for work performed in your current field while in the military. It has to directly relate to what you're doing, so say you were a JAG in the Army, and then get a position as a civilian attorney for the government, then you may be eligible to get credit for all of that time you were a JAG. You have to be able to provide documentation showing that your prior duties were directly related to the duties you will be performing in your new federal career. Your annual evaluations should be sufficient. This is not a guarantee like the previous leave accrual benefit and due to it's frustratingly similar name, it becomes quickly confused with the other benefit. This incentive **MUST** be requested prior to EOD otherwise your HR does not even need to consider it. It **CANNOT** be performed retroactively. That requirement about not being able to be requested after you start (and probably learn about the program) is the sneaky ridiculousness of the incentive. How do you request something you don't even know about? If you know about it, this incentive can really move the ball on your leave accrual date.

There are two OPM web pages on the subjects above. The Creditable Service for Leave Accrual can be found at https://www.opm.gov/policy-data-oversight/data-analysis-documentation/personnel-documentation/servicecreditleave.pdf. This one is pretty straight forward. The second, further amended portion of that same policy, the Creditable Service for Annual Leave Accrual for Non-Federal Work Experience and Experience in the Uniformed Service, can be found at https://www.opm.gov/policy-data-oversight/pay-leave/leave-administration/fact-sheets/creditable-service-for-annual-leave-accrual-for-non-federal-work-experience-and-experience-in-the-uniformed-service/.

The Uniform

What to wear to a job interview is often a source of debate and you'll never be able to make another first impression. The absolute best advice that I can give you is that there is no such thing as being overdressed for an interview. However, you can absolutely be underdressed. If possible, get an idea of the daily attire of employees through their website or from personal observation. If the employees wear jeans and t-shirts to work every day, go up a level with a nice shirt or blouse and a pressed pair of pants or skirt. If they wear collared shirts and slacks, go with a suit.

As styles change and evolve it would be impossible to say that what is appropriate today will remain so tomorrow. As such, I recommend you spend some time on the internet researching the various types of dress, such as smart casual, business casual, business professional, and business formal.

FINAL THOUGHTS

As I mentioned in the beginning, this guide is nowhere near a comprehensive list of every resource, tool, or trick out there when navigating the Army's retirement process. It's based on my personal experiences with, and research into, the topic. For example, you may find that the Retirement Services folks at your installation are really good at their jobs and care about the soldiers who've dedicated their entire adult lives up to that point in service to our nation. Or you may have an instructor at SFL-TAP that knows everything about the VA and can do more than read the slides line-by-line and can give clear guidance on how to begin the VA disability process. It just wasn't my experience with the system.

You may or may not be struggling with whether to apply for VA benefits during your transition period. Trust me on this one, I get it. I didn't join the Army when I was 18 with the belief that I'd be eligible for federal benefits my whole life. That's crazy. My dad served for 22 years, he didn't file a VA claim. It's just not something that a lot of people did back in the day. Whether you file a claim or not, please insure you stay enrolled in the VA system in some way. There are potential illnesses that have yet to be diagnosed based on things that we, as veterans, have been exposed to—especially if you deployed to the Middle East during your career.

Throughout this guide, I tried to keep the commentary somewhat lighthearted as the process can often be frustrating. I truly hope that you've been able to glean a little bit of knowledge from my experiences. I promise that I'm not as jaded as my sarcastic humor may appear to be, and I'm extremely proud of my service.

You should be as well. You may feel like you're just another cog in the big Army machine, but you have accomplished something that very few people actually have. You've made a career out of self-sacrifice. Now, go enjoy your retirement!

Grunt Style t-shirt design that captures the spirit of
retirement perfectly.

RESOURCES

Here's a list of resources. The web links were valid at the time of publication.

General Retirement Resources

Retirement benefits calculator, plus a lot of other valuable resources:

https://myarmybenefits.us.army.mil/Benefit-Calculators/Retirement

https://soldierforlife.army.mil/Retirement/retirement-planning

HRC Enlisted Retirements and Separations Branch page:
https://www.hrc.army.mil/content/Regular%20Army%20Enlisted%20Retirements%20and%20Separations

DoD Transportation: www.move.mil

SFL-TAP

https://portal.sfl-tap.army.mil/ACAP_WEB/onlineCLMenuPage.do

DFAS

MyPay: https://mypay.dfas.mil/#/

Phone number: 1 (888) 332-7411

Information on CRSC and CRDP:

https://www.dfas.mil/retiredmilitary/disability/payment.html

Comparing CRSC and CRDP:

https://www.dfas.mil/retiredmilitary/disability/comparison.html

Tricare Online:

https://www.tricareonline.com/tol2/protected/shared/home.xhtml

Veterans Affairs

Main site: www.VA.gov

VA eBenefits: www.eBenefits.VA.gov

Comprehensive VA Benefits Document (52 pages):

https://www.benefits.va.gov/REPORTS/abr/docs/2019-compensation.pdf

VA Welcome Kit: https://www.va.gov/welcome-kit/

VA Combined Ratings Table: https://www.va.gov/VA-combined-ratings-table-2019.pdf

VA Disability Dependent Claim:
https://benefits.va.gov/COMPENSATION/docs/bas-dependency-faq-final-508.pdf

VA Yellow Ribbon Program:
https://www.va.gov/education/about-gi-bill-benefits/post-9-11/yellow-ribbon-program/

VA Healthcare: https://www.va.gov/health-care/eligibility/

VA Burn Pit Registry:
https://veteran.mobilehealth.va.gov/AHBurnPitRegistry/

VA Combined list of Benefits:
https://www.reddit.com/r/VeteransBenefits/wiki/combinedbenefits?utm_source=share&utm_medium=ios_app&utm_name=iossmf

Finances

State Income Tax Information:

https://militarybenefits.info/states-that-do-dont-tax-military-retirement-pay/

Selling Leave: https://www.military.com/military-transition/personal-finances/should-you-sell-back-leave-or-take-terminal-leave.html#:~:text=Selling%20Back%20Leave&text=You%20are%20entitled%20to%20sell,varying%20amounts%20for%20state%20tax

Civilian Careers

Great resume tips for translating military jargon to civilian language:

https://news.clearancejobs.com/2010/05/10/common-military-to-civilian-translations/

Federal Hiring Authorities:

https://www.fedshirevets.gov/job-seekers/veterans/special-hiring-authorities/

Website specifically targeting Vets for working in the federal service:
www.FedsHireVets.gov

USAJobs (federal civilian): www.usajobs.gov

ClearanceJobs (mostly contracting, some federal jobs listed): www.clearancejobs.com

ClearedJobs (headhunting company specializing in the DC area): www.clearedjobs.net

Military Federal Jobs Crosswalk. Translate your MOS into federal civilian job series:
https://www.dllr.state.md.us/mil2fedjobs/

Buying back military time website:
https://www.dfas.mil/civilianemployees/militaryservice/militaryservicedeposits/estimator/

Civilian Leave Accrual Benefits and Incentives:
https://www.opm.gov/policy-data-oversight/data-analysis-documentation/personnel-documentation/servicecreditleave.pdf

https://www.opm.gov/policy-data-oversight/pay-leave/leave-administration/fact-sheets/creditable-service-for-annual-leave-accrual-for-non-federal-work-experience-and-experience-in-the-uniformed-service/

RETIREMENT CHECKLIST

This isn't all-inclusive, but it's pretty darn good considering there isn't an official retirement checklist.

Retirement Packet

- ☐ Prepare memorandums requesting retirement and adherence to SHARP.
- ☐ Retirement Award write up (DA638).
- ☐ DA4187 requesting retirement.
- ☐ Submit PTDY and Transition Leave. They need to be separated by at least two weeks, otherwise you'll get your clearing papers while on PTDY.

Military Medical

- ☐ Get your injuries and illnesses documented in your medical records!!
- ☐ Request copy of medical records – leave time for yourself due to "clerical errors".
- ☐ Make a copy of the disk and print the records.
- ☐ Schedule your Army physical no earlier than 6 months prior to the start of your transition leave. This is mandatory for retirement.
- ☐ Request a TRICARE Online account and link your Patient Secure Messaging to it.

☐ Call TRICARE prior to the 2nd day of the month prior to when you retire to ensure your medical coverage doesn't lapse.

☐ Have enough prescription medication to last you at least a month after retirement while all the coverages switch over from Active Duty to Retiree.

SFL-TAP

☐ Schedule your online/telephonic interview (18-24 months out).

☐ Schedule initial face-to-face with an SFL-TAP counselor (NET 12 months out).

☐ Schedule the 5-day, in-person course at an SFL-TAP center.

☐ Attend any classes offered that seem interesting or of use for your post-retirement life.

☐ Arrange to have the first O-6 in your chain of command sign the DD2648.

☐ Complete your CAPSTONE appointment to receive the final, completed DD2648 with a counselor stating you've completed the program requirements.

☐ Hold onto the DD2648 because you'll need it at your Final Out appointment.

Retirement Services

- ☐ Schedule the MANDATORY Pre-Retirement Brief.
- ☐ Receive your retirement orders.
- ☐ Contact Retirement Services to get a working copy of your DD214—go over this document thoroughly, make sure it is 100% correct.
- ☐ Turn in of your DD2648.
- ☐ Survivor Benefit Plan (SBP) election (NET 60 days prior to the start of your transition leave). If you decide not to take it, your spouse **MUST** attend with you. After SBP election, you're transferred to the Transition Assistance office.

Transition Services

- ☐ Receive installation clearing papers 2-weeks prior to the start date of your Transition Leave.
- ☐ Schedule Final Out appointment with Finance.
- ☐ Get unit clearing papers from your S-1.
- ☐ Clear CIF (must be in uniform).
- ☐ You've done this a lot of times before. Follow the clearing papers instructions.
- ☐ Final Out is the day before your Transition Leave begins.

Other

- ☐ Ensure your DEERS is accurate.

- ☐ Request to transfer your Post-9/11 GI Bill eligibility prior to separation.
- ☐ Get a username and PIN for your MyPay before you retire, while you still have your CAC.
- ☐ Establish a DS Logon account.
- ☐ Prepare a Statement of Service for your commander to sign if you plan on working in the federal government.
- ☐ If you plan on becoming a government contractor, you'll need the DoD Ethics letter prepared by the installation JAG.
- ☐ Verify with your S-1 that they have your flag and retirement certificate.
- ☐ Schedule an appointment with your local ID Card office for you <u>and</u> your family members before you transition.
- ☐ You have up to 5 years for your final military move. You must renew eligibility each year.

Personal

- ☐ Spouse and family prepared to leave the military support network.
- ☐ Financially prepared to retire – Final Pay can be 6 weeks or more from last day of Active Duty.
- ☐ Research locations for retirement home, determine tax implications.
- ☐ Decide if you want to work after you retire from the military.

VA Medical Info

- ☐ Request an eBenefits account.
- ☐ Get a VSO.
- ☐ Put together your working copy of ailments, ideally each of them will have documentation in your medical records.
- ☐ Immerse yourself on the various VA websites and learn all you can.
- ☐ Schedule appointment with your VSO 180-90 days out from retirement date.
- ☐ Gather the paperwork required by the VA when your VSO submits your packet.
  - DD214 Worksheet; plus any additional DD214 you may have.
  - Printed copy of your medical records (bring a CD copy just in case they update their archaic methods between the time I wrote this and when you retire).
  - Printed copy of Retirement Physical.
  - Bank account routing information.
  - Marriage certificate and divorce decrees (if applicable).
  - Birth certificates of children.
  - Records that indicate you are the primary care giver for adult dependents (if applicable).
- ☐ Wait (and then wait some more).
- ☐ Schedule your VA Compensation and Pension Exam (their version of a physical).
- ☐ Check your claim status on the VA.gov website.

- [ ] Attend **EVERY** appointment requested by the VA. Do not skip any, no matter how good your excuse may seem.
- [ ] Once you receive your disability rating, double check using the combined ratings table, determine if it makes sense. If not, file an appeal.